How to Write Essays

For GCSE English Literature

Neil Bowen

Published by pushmepress.com an imprint of Inducit Learning Ltd

Pawlett House, West Street, Somerton,

Somerset TA11 7PS, United Kingdom

www.pushmepress.com

First published in 2013

ISBN: 978-1-909618-20-6

Contents

Introduction

This book is organised into the following five sections:

1. Understanding the assessment objectives

2. Understanding what examiners are looking for: a hierarchy of grades from D to A*

3. Planning essays

4. Writing essays

5. Exemplar essays

This book aims to take you on a learning journey, a journey which helps you develop your knowledge of the skills necessary to write excellent GCSE Literature essays. Along the way you will have a chance to develop your reading and writing skills. As we travel, we need to take careful note of the details of what we experience.

We will start off by explaining and examining the significance of the assessment objectives used by all the examination boards. From there we will go on to explore the nature of mark schemes. In the next section of the book we'll examine the best strategies for planning essays, turning "brainstorming" into logical sequences of ideas. Then we will arrive at the writing process itself. In this section we will look at writing style, register and technical vocabulary. Our final destination will help us explore work written by students in real examination conditions. Here you'll find exemple essays ranging from C grade to A.

There is no single, correct way to write a Literature essay. Writing frames have become popular teaching tools and sometimes these imply that there is only one way to answer a question. You may be familiar with essay-writing frames like the following:

1. Introduction: Write about the context of the book

2. Write about the importance of the central character

3. Write about how this character relates to other characters

4. Write about the language in the book

5. Conclusion: Explain what you think of the book.

Though they have their uses as a way of helping you to structure your writing, such frames can also restrict the writer and often they appear random and arbitrary. Why, for example, should we write about a main character in the second paragraph? An overly rigid approach leads to essays that seem mechanical, essays in which GCSE pupils dutifully work through a pre-set agenda.

You will do much better and achieve higher grades if you learn how to write your own essays, following a structure you have deliberately chosen as a means to convey your own ideas about a text. Of course, your essays must be informed by the work you do with your peers and the advice of your teachers. And there are rules to learn about how to write effectively about texts. But fundamentally, your literary essays should be expressing your own thinking in your own voice and style. So, we ask you to take a deep breath and embrace the freedom.

The aim of this book is to provide you with all you need to know about how to write great GCSE English Literature essays. We explore the key background information of how exam boards mark your work and then show you how to plan and write your essays. At each stage of the way we will use examples from real GCSE Literature essays to help make what you need to do as clear as possible.

This book aims to take you on a road to excellence. We'll begin our journey with the key ideas underpinning marking of all GCSE Literature essays, the assessment objectives.

Understanding the assessment objectives

Imagine you're in the changing rooms before a sports fixture. You're tying the laces on your boots, fitting the shin guards, straightening your collar, checking your shoulder pads and your helmet. You pick up your racket, your stick and your bat, or put your riding crop under your arm. Now you jog out onto the field, the court, the pitch or the ground.

You have no idea what sport you're playing. You've no idea what the rules are. You've no idea what offside means, how you achieve marks for artistic impression, even how you score a goal, a penalty, a try or a point. How are you going to win this game?

It's obvious you're not going to win. And, when the match is over, unsurprisingly your performance on the field has indeed been very poor. Now switch the field to an examination hall.

But many, perhaps even the majority of pupils, enter the exam hall ready to face an English Literature exam paper without any real idea of how this particular game works, how points are earned or what the judges are looking for.

To illustrate this, try writing down now, from memory, the assessment objectives for the English Literature GCSE you are taking. Ask yourself are you playing the 'sport' of English Literature without really understanding the rules of the game?

If you don't know what assessment objectives are, or you weren't even aware that they existed, then you need to read this book. If you're one of the few pupils who do know the assessment objectives now, then try writing down the mark scheme the examiners will use to access your performance. If you don't know the marks scheme you will also benefit from reading this book. If you are one of the few pupils who could do both, you may think you don't need to read this book.

But even if you already know and understand the rules of the game, this book will help you develop the skills to succeed.

ASSESSMENT OBJECTIVES

All the exam boards, Edexcel, AQA, CIE, OCR, WJEC use these same four assessment objectives to underpin marking of all GCSE Literature essays. That includes the marking of examinations, controlled assessments and coursework:

- **AO1** - Respond to texts critically and imaginatively; select and evaluate relevant textual detail to illustrate and support interpretations

- **AO2** - Explain how language, structure and form contribute to writers' presentation of ideas, themes and settings

- **AO3** - Make comparisons and explain links between texts, evaluating writers' different ways of expressing meaning and achieving effects

- **AO4** - Relate texts to their social, cultural and historical contexts; explain how texts have been influential and significant to self and other readers in different contexts and at different times.

Boiling this information down a little we can say that to succeed on your English Literature GCSE you will have to:

- **AO1** - Develop a critical approach, using evidence well

- **AO2** - Analyse language closely

- **AO3** - Compare texts carefully

- **AO4** - Explore the contexts and the significance of texts.

These assessment objectives can be achieved at different levels. An exploration of a text's significance at C grade will look very different from at E or A grade. To understand how the assessment objectives translate into grades we need therefore to look closely at mark schemes. This will helps us to appreciate the skills examiners are looking for.

There are only four assessment objectives. Make sure that you know and understand them. If you can, have them to hand when you are writing practice essays.

Understanding what examiners are really looking for ...

The next stage in our journey leads us to a closer focus on the key skills you need to develop to write a top quality Literature essay. Here is a sample of an English Literature GCSE mark scheme for the most widely studied specification, AQA. Mark schemes for Edexcel, and for Cambridge IGCSE and for AQA controlled assessments can be found at the back of this book in appendix 1. The WJEC (the Welsh Board) marking criteria are available on their website.

A word of warning; the Bands don't translate directly into grades. But broadly Band 3 is around a C grade, Band 4 approximately equates to a B grade, Band 5 is about an A and Band 6 roughly equals an A*.

AQA examination mark schemes are available on the board's website. They provide marking criteria for responses from Band 1 up to Band 6. If you read from Band 1 onwards you should be able to trace the increasing level of skill and understanding required as you move up the grades.

AQA LITERATURE EXAMINATION MARK SCHEME

Mark Band 1

Candidates demonstrate:

- Simple response to task and to the text

- Reference to some details

- Reference to writer's methods

- Simple comment on meaning(s)

- Despite frequent lapses in syntax and spelling, meaning can be derived

Mark Band 2

Candidates demonstrate:

- Some clear response to task and to the text

- Range of details used

- Simple identification of method(s)

- Some range of explicit meanings given

- Syntax and spelling are sufficiently clear to convey meaning

Mark Band 3

Candidates demonstrate:

- Supported response to task and to the text

- Comment(s) on detail(s)

- Awareness of writer making choice(s) of language and/or structure and/or form

- Generalisations about ideas/themes/feelings/attitudes

- Despite lapses, information is presented in a way which is usually clear. Syntax and spelling have some degree of accuracy, although there are likely to be frequent errors

Mark Band 4

Candidates demonstrate:

- Explained response to task and to the text

- Details used to support a range of comments

- Identification of effect(s) of writer's choices of language and/or form and/or structure

- Awareness of ideas/themes/feelings/attitudes

- Information is presented in a way which is generally clear. Syntax and spelling have some degree of accuracy

Mark Band 5

Candidates demonstrate:

- Sustained response to task and to the text

- Effective use of details to support interpretation

- Explanation of effects of writer's uses of language and/or structure and/or form

- Understanding of themes/ideas

- Information is usually presented in a way which assists with communication of meaning. Syntax and spelling are generally accurate

Mark Band 6

Candidates demonstrate:

- Considered/qualified response to task and to the text

- Details linked to interpretation

- Appreciation/consideration of writer's uses of language and/or form and/or structure and effect on readers/audience

- Thoughtful consideration of ideas/themes

- Information is presented in a way which assists with communication of meaning. Syntax and spelling are generally accurate

Although the assessment objectives underpin marking of all forms of assessment for GCSE Literature, examination marks schemes are slightly different to the controlled assessment ones. This is because the assessment objectives are not spread evenly across all the forms of assessment. For instance, on the AQA Unit 1 examination paper there is no comparative task and so **AO3** (make comparisons and explain links between texts, evaluating writers' different ways of expressing meaning and achieving effects) is not tested on this paper. On AQA Unit 2 AO3 is tested through the comparison of poems.

Each exam board distributes assessment objectives differently across their specifications. There is not space in this book to go through how all the assessment objectives are weighted, and to compare all the different systems would be very confusing. But we strongly recommend that for each Literature essay you write you find out which assessment objectives are the most important. To do this you can either look on the exam board's website or simply ask your English teacher.

Approximate grade and key qualities of candidates' work

E - Simple response to ideas and techniques, frequent errors.

D - Some understanding of straightforward ideas and techniques.

C - Clear understanding of writers' choices as well as of some ideas and techniques.

B - Detailed understanding of the effects of writers' choices, as well as a range of ideas and techniques.

A - Sustained, detailed explanation of writers' choices, as well as key ideas and techniques.

A* - Detailed appreciation and interpretation of writers' choices, as well as of thoughtful consideration of key ideas and techniques.

To move from a B to an A or A* grade you have to choose more carefully the material you analyse - that is what is meant by 'discriminating'. You also have to be perceptive, which means reading beyond the obvious or the surface layer, and you need to evaluate. This means weighing up the success of the choices writers have made.

In their specifications all the examination boards also have another go at defining the characteristics of candidates' performances at different levels of achievement. A couple of examples from Edexcel and AQA boards should help clarify the picture.

GRADE DESCRIPTORS

Edexcel

‣ A grade

Candidates respond enthusiastically and critically to texts, showing imagination and originality in developing alternative approaches and interpretations. They confidently explore and evaluate how language, structure and form contribute to writers' varied ways of presenting ideas, themes and settings, and how they achieve specific effects on readers. Candidates make illuminating connections and comparisons between texts. They identify and comment on the impact of the social, cultural and historical contexts of texts on different readers at different times. They convey ideas persuasively and cogently, supporting them with apt textual references.

‣ C grade

Candidates understand and demonstrate how writers use ideas, themes and settings in texts to affect the reader. They respond personally to the effects of language, structure and form, referring to textual detail to support their views and reactions. They explain the relevance and impact of connections and comparisons between texts. They show awareness of some of the social, cultural and historical contexts of texts and of how this influences their meanings for contemporary and modern readers. They convey ideas clearly and appropriately.

‣ E grade

Candidates make an involved, personal response to the effects of language, structure and form in texts, showing some awareness of key ideas, themes or arguments. They support their views by reference to significant features or details. They make straightforward connections and comparisons between texts and suggest how this contributes to readers' understanding and enjoyment. They are aware that some aspects of texts relate to their specific social, cultural and historical contexts, and suggest successfully why this may be significant with reference to some texts.

AQA

▸ A grade

Candidates respond enthusiastically and critically to texts, showing imagination and originality in developing alternative approaches and interpretations. They confidently explore and evaluate how language, structure and form contribute to writers' varied ways of presenting ideas, themes and settings, and how they achieve specific effects on readers. Candidates make illuminating connections and comparisons between texts. They identify and comment on the impact of the social, cultural and historical contexts of texts on different readers at different times. They convey ideas persuasively and cogently, supporting them with apt textual references.

▸ C grade

Candidates understand and demonstrate how writers use ideas, themes and settings in texts to affect the reader. They respond personally to the effects of language, structure and form, referring to textual detail to support their views and reactions. They explain the relevance and impact of connections and comparisons between texts. They show awareness of some of the social, cultural and historical contexts of texts and of how this influences their meanings for contemporary and modern readers. They convey ideas clearly and appropriately

▸ **E grade**

Candidates make an involved, personal response to the effects of language, structure and form in texts, showing some awareness of key ideas, themes or arguments. They support their views by reference to significant features or details. They make straightforward connections and comparisons between texts and suggest how this contributes to readers' understanding and enjoyment. They are aware that some aspects of texts relate to their specific social, cultural and historical contexts, and suggest successfully why this may be significant with reference to some texts.

No doubt you will have worked out that these descriptors are the same for both boards! This underlines the point that though their wording might be a bit different at times and their choice of the weighting they give to an assessment objective on a single essay might vary, fundamentally all the boards are looking for the same skills and qualities.

Summary

Make sure that you look up and read mark schemes. Check what the weighting is for each assessment objective on each essay you have to write.

We've now studied the assessment information and familiarised ourselves with the 'rules of the game' and what the examiners are looking for in your essays. Our next section will explore how to plan essays effectively.

Planning your essays

The elements of planning a successful Literature essay can be broken down into two related aspects:

1. Thinking about Literary texts: brainstorming & planning

2. Structuring your writing; introductions, conclusions, paragraphing

THE THINKING & PLANNING STAGE

For a coursework piece, or a controlled assessment, you have time to really think about the material you must cover in your essay. In exam conditions, however, you have only between 5 and 10 minutes to brainstorm and plan your essay. In the exam you will feel under pressure to begin writing. It's important to resist this urge. You must give yourself a reasonable amount of thinking and planning time.

Weak answers tend to be overly focused on re-telling the story of the texts: this happened and then this happened and then this happened. If you find yourself writing phrases such as 'and then' or 'when this' or 'when that' often in your essay you will know that you're writing a narrative summary and consequently you won't be scoring many marks. Examiners expect you to know the chronology of events in your texts; they don't want you simply to demonstrate that you can remember what happened. They're interested in what you think about the ideas raised in the text and the techniques writers use.

Good answers focus on the question set and answer it by advancing a number of connected points. These points are explored in some detail through the close analysis of quotations and other specific details from the texts.

The nature of literary texts

All Literature texts and all Literature exam questions explore two main features of novels, plays, short stories and poems: what the text is about and how it is written.

What the text is about refers to the content of the text, the ideas, experiences or emotions it explores or describes. How it is written focuses on the writer's technique. By technique we mean the craft of the writing, the linguistic (language) and structural devices a writer uses, as well as their creation of characters and use of settings.

In different types of literary writing, such as poems, plays, novels and short stories, the writer can use different techniques. For a poet linquistic devices might include metaphor and symbol; for a novelist or a playwright they will include characterisation and dialogue. Structural devices in a poem include stanzas, in a novel chapters, and in a play scenes.

Consider how writing a play would present different challenges to writing a novel. For instance, why is it easier for a novelist to move their characters through multiple settings than it is for a playwright? It's because changing the stage during a performance in a theatre is difficult. That is why changes of stage set in plays often happen at the ends of acts. In a novel, changing a setting is easy and can happen in one sentence: 'John sat at his computer typing his essay. Meanwhile on a distant planet...'

A novelist can use a narrator to provide information on a character. Although a playwright does not have this facility, he or she will, however, have actors who can bring dialogue to life, adding tone, expressions and actions. Clearly they have features in common, but novels and plays are very different art forms. In a weak essay these differences are often ignored, and both types of texts are simply called 'books'.

So it's vital that you distinguish sharply between them and show understanding of the nature and demands of the different art forms.

When you are brainstorming a question try to think first in terms of what the text is about and how it is written. In all Literature the style and technique of writing is closely connected to thematic concerns. To achieve the higher grades you need to explore how these two aspects relate to each other, in other words, how a writer's choices of technique connect to what they are writing about.

Thinking about what the text is about will also help you to consider other important questions:

1. What is the purpose of the text?

2. What context was it written in?

3. Does the text fit into a genre?

Putting this together, the key questions we need to ask ourselves about any Literature text are:

1. What type of text is this?

a. A poem, a play, a short story or novel?

b. What is its genre? A ghost story, a protest novel, a love poem, a tragedy or a comedy?

2. What is the text about? What are its thematic concerns?

3. What is/was the writer's purpose?

4. What are the key techniques they use?

5. When and where was the text written?

From your classroom study of the Literature set texts you should have developed a good sense of the answers to the above questions. Once you have thought carefully about each of these you are then ready to address the specific question you have been given.

Mindmaps are an excellent way to help you order your thoughts. For example, you can watch the You Tube clip, 'Maximise the power of your brain' with Tony Buzan to find out how they can work for you.

Different types of Literature Questions

What type of questions do examiners ask about literary texts? What are the rules of this particular game? A simple way to familiarise yourself with the sorts of questions you're likely to have to answer in your GCSE is to try writing some yourself.

Questions like 'What did George say to Lennie on p.55?', 'Is 'Lord of the Flies' a good book?' or 'What's the point of reading a play?' might be of some interest, but these aren't the sorts of questions you're likely to face in an English GCSE exam.

In fact, Literature questions fall into **FOUR** main categories:

1. Questions focusing on a specific character. For example, Discuss the significance of the character of Piggy in 'Lord of the Flies'.

2. Questions on the relationships between characters: Explore the significance of the relationship between George and Lennie in 'Of Mice and Men'.

3. Questions focusing on a major theme: Examine what Priestley suggests about moral responsibility in 'An Inspector Calls'.

4. Questions focusing on technique or the effects of writing: Examine how the poet uses language powerfully in the poem.

CHARACTER and **CHARACTER RELATIONSHIP** based questions tend to be the most popular with GCSE pupils. The essential thing with this type of question is to think of what a character contributes to the text in terms of plot and themes. Then think about how they are presented by the writer.

Do not simply write everything you know about the character.

The following diagram gives you the ten most important questions to ask when examining a character from a work of fiction:

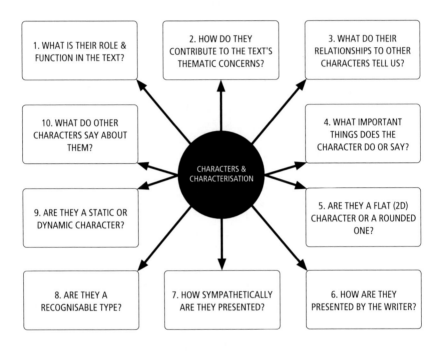

Each of these questions can be explored in more detail.

1. Are they the protagonist (main character)? A reliable witness? The villain? What status do they have in their world?

2. For example, the theme of prejudice in 'Of Mice and Men' is explored through the experiences of Crooks (who is black in a white world), Curley's wife (who is a woman in a man's world), Lennie (who is mentally backward in an uncaring world) and Candy (who is disabled in an uncaring world).

3. Who are their friends and their enemies? Who do they talk to,

confide in, spend time with?

4. Are there any differences between their words and actions?

5. Do we believe in them as people (rounded) or are they thinly presented because they serve the plot?

6. Are we told what they look like? Are we given access to their thoughts? Do we find out biographical details, such as their age, their family, where they come from? Do we learn about them from their actions? What language do they use? How do they speak and think?

7. Are we meant to like them? Are we at least meant to empathise with them?

8. How should we react to common literary types such as the mad scientist, the detective with a drink problem, the femme fatale or the gentle giant?

9. Does the story change them? If so, how and by how much? What do they learn?

10. How are they treated by other characters? Are they respected or despised, treated with suspicion or trusted, loved or loathed?

Tackling a thematic question

What exactly is a theme?

This may seem like a question with an obvious answer. But many GCSE and 'A' level students are rather hazy about the definition of a theme. So, here's a clear definition for you: a theme is a subject returned to repeatedly in any literary text, an idea that the writer explores in their work. Generally themes are abstract, such as love, death, loneliness, justice, prejudice, social responsibility.

Motifs are not themes. Motifs are repeated patterns of language or imagery in a literary work. In 'Lord of the Flies' the 'conch' is used before characters speak at a gathering. In 'Of Mice and Men' various animals repeatedly appear. These are motifs, not themes. Many pupils confuse these two terms.

Motifs can, and often do, have thematic significance. The conch symbolises order and civilisation, for example, and the animals symbolise vulnerability to exploitation and violence.

A final example: In Shakespeare's dark tragedy, 'Macbeth', the playwright explores the theme of deception. When Lady Macbeth advises her husband to cover up his plan to murder the King, she says 'look like the innocent flower, but be the serpent under't'. Later she tells him that he must disguise his thoughts as his face is like a 'book' in which men can read his intentions. Physical things, such as flowers, serpents and books can be motifs, but they are not themes. The theme they convey in 'Macbeth' is deception.

▸ Identifying vs. exploring themes

Often in examination papers pupils simply identify themes and leave their comments at that. For instance, in essays on the theme of love in 'Romeo and Juliet' many pupils write something along the following lines:

Intro:

> *'In this essay I am going to explore how Shakespeare presents the theme of love. I will write about how this is mainly done through the presentation of the characters of Romeo and Juliet themselves. But there are also other types of love in the play, such as the friendship love of Romeo and Mercutio and love of family, as shown by Tybalt, which I will also explore.*

Characteristically these sorts of essays then go on to list the different presentations of love in the play, along the lines of the following:

1st paragraph

> *At the start of the play Romeo thinks he is in love with Rosalind, but he isn't really, he is in love with the idea of being in love...'*

2nd & 3rd paragraphs

> *It is only when he meets Juliet that Romeo really falls in genuine love. This is shown by the beautiful language Shakespeare gives the characters...this sort of love is the highly romantic, love-at-first-sight type of love familiar from Hollywood films.*

4th paragraph

> *However, this isn't the only type of love explored in the play. Shakespeare also writes about love within families, between parents and children, and love of the idea of family..*

Typically the essay will end pretty much where it began...

> *I have now shown that Shakespeare explores lots of different types of love, including...*

This sort of cataloguing approach earns pupils a solid D grade. With some comments on language it might rise to a C. Stop and think how this essay could be improved.

A good way to approach this task would be to consider what questions the essay leaves unanswered. The biggest of these, surely, is what does Shakespeare have to say about love? It's all very well saying he writes about love, but the essential question is what do we actually learn about the nature of love from the play?

Just some of the supplementary questions we could include would be: what is Shakespeare's attitude to love? How does he define love? How does love affect people's behaviour? What is the value of love? Is Shakespeare saying love is always a good thing? Are there bad types of love? What if you love money, or property, or violence? How close are love and hate? Can love easily become hate? Can you have love without hate? How easy is it to distinguish love from lust, or from madness? Is love a sort of disease or a curse? Is it true that 'all you need is love'?

Questions of this nature address what exam boards refer to as the 'significance' of texts.

If you want to write a top grade essay, it is not enough to say the writer writes about a particular theme; you have to explore what conclusions their novel/poem/play suggests about it.

As we will see later in this book, essay style is very important to your chances of achieving a good grade. In the sample introduction above, the candidate writes, 'in this essay I am going to write about...' Though examination boards do not explicitly penalise this style we recommend that you avoid it.

Why?

Firstly, because you are wasting time telling the reader what you are going to do, when you should just get on and do it. Secondly, because you are telling your reader what they have already gathered from your essay's title. Therefore this sort of phrase is redundant and worth zero marks.

In addition to questions on characters, theme and style, there are four other common types of questions found on GCSE examination papers:

1. Most exam boards include a comparative question somewhere on their Literature paper. Often, but not always, they choose the poetry for a comparative task.

2. Some exam boards include an unseen poetry question, where you have to analyse a poem you're reading for the first time.

3. A number of exam boards include extract-based questions that require close reading of the writer's technique.

4. Only one exam board, CIE, includes an empathetic response, where you have to write as if you were a character in a text.

Sometimes this sort of question is set for coursework.

We will come on to how you should tackle these less common types of Literature essay later. For now we want to focus on the single text question. Now let's try to apply these ideas to a specific example question.

The Literature texts which feature most often across the different exam boards are John Steinbeck's 'Of Mice and Men' and 'An Inspector Calls' by J.B. Priestley. So we will use these texts as the main focus for examples. Don't worry if you aren't studying either of these. The principles of great GCSE Literature essays are the same whatever the text. For the poetry questions we're going to use a poem by William Blake called 'The Sick Rose'. We're not using this because it crops up a lot on lots of examination boards' specifications. We're using it because it's one of the greatest poems ever written by one of our greatest poets. It's also very short.

‣ 'The Sick Rose' (first published 1794)

O Rose thou art sick.

The invisible worm,

That flies in the night

In the howling storm:

Has found out thy bed

Of crimson joy:

And his dark secret love

Does thy life destroy.

Some sample questions in the style of exam boards:

- **PROSE** - Explore the significance of loneliness in Steinbeck's 'Of Mice and Men'

- **DRAMA** - Examine the significance of the role of Eva Smith in Priestley's 'An Inspector Calls'

- **POETRY** - Explore the ways in which Blake employs language in his poem to create a powerful impact

What type of question is the first one on prose? Clearly it is a thematic question focusing on a major concern of Steinbeck's novel. The best way to tackle this sort of question is to consider how the various techniques the novelist uses contribute to the exploration of loneliness:

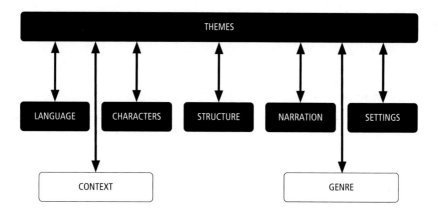

We can add genre and contexts as factors which shape the nature of the novel.

In fact this is a useful way of thinking about any Literature question – how do the micro (small scale) details of language relate to the macro (large scale) level of thematic concerns.

Imagine the text is a photograph of a landscape. Another way of thinking of the process is that you have to both zoom in, to examine details, and then zoom out to put these into the context of the whole panorama.

For the 'Of Mice and Men' question our brainstorm might look something like this:

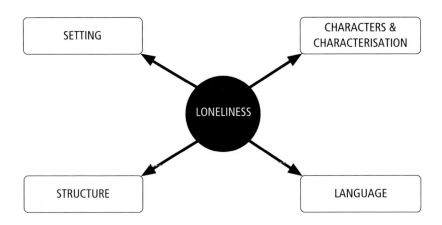

▸ **Setting**

The bunkhouse is a hostile, isolating context. Crooks is segregated; he has a separate room from the others.

▸ **Characters & Characterisation**

Almost all the characters except George and Lennie are lonely; Curley's wife, Candy, Crooks especially. How is their loneliness shown? What are the causes of their loneliness? Curley's wife is the only woman, Candy loses the only thing he loved, his dog, Crooks is isolated because of his colour. The boss and Slim tell us that few men mix with each other.

‣ Language

The name of the town 'Soledad' means 'loneliness' in Spanish. The characters play the game 'solitaire'. In the dream George tells Lennie, he contrasts their friendship with how isolated other men are from each other. Contrasts between friendship and loneliness run through the novel.

‣ Structure

The cyclical nature of the novel implies the characters are doomed to repeat the same lonely patterns. The single chapter on Crooks is also cyclical, indicating he is isolated and trapped.

In addition to this we also need to think about Steinbeck's purpose as well as the context and genre of the novel. 'Of Mice and Men' is a protest novel and Steinbeck is trying to make the reader feel sympathetic to poor migrant workers who suffered so badly during the Great Depression. The loneliness of the characters is caused mainly by the harsh, dog-eat-dog world they live in. By describing their loneliness Steinbeck makes us feel sympathy.

We should also consider narration. Arguably Steinbeck's restricted third person narrator is separated from the characters, but it is as if by telling the story he can feel closer to these characters.

From this brainstorm we can see that the main focus of our essay will be on characters and characterisation, as this is the major tool Steinbeck uses to explore the theme of loneliness. So, what is now emerging is a **ROUGH PLAN**. Our next task will be to put the material into a logical sequence or structure.

For the 'An Inspector Calls' the brainstorming might be something along the lines of:

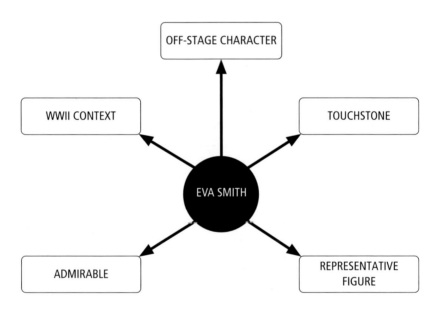

Eva Smith is an **OFF-STAGE** character, but still crucial to Priestley's purposes

She functions as a **TOUCHSTONE**; other characters' personalities and behaviour are revealed through their treatment of her (arguably the major part of her role in the play). Mr Birling, for example, is shown to be an arrogant, self-centred snob and a greedy, exploitative employer. Crucially, he and Mrs Birling deny responsibility and feel no compassion, in contrast to Gerald, Sheila and Eric. Therefore reaction to Eva falls into two patterns.

Eva Smith is a **REPRESENTATIVE** figure - the working classes and the downtrodden. Her tragic story is used by Priestley to change middle class audiences' attitudes and sympathies to the poor.

Through the Inspector she is also shown to have **ADMIRABLE** qualities in contrast to the Birlings - courage, fortitude, resilience etc - e.g. in the protecting of Eric - increasing our sympathy.

Written just after the end of **WWII** the play is encouraging the nation to pull together and rebuild society in a better, fairer way. It is a didactic play, a modern morality tale. Eva Smith = abused virtue. The detective aspect makes the morality palatable for the audience. Eva Smith = role of the murdered innocent.

A common mistake when writing about **POETRY** is for candidates to work through a poem chronologically or sequentially. After the introduction the following paragraph will start with something like:

In the first verse the poet tries to say that…

And the paragraphs that follow will continue to follow the order of the poem:

In the second verse the poem is about...

In the third verse the poet uses a metaphor....

Mistakes to Avoid

Firstly, as we have already said, you are not being asked to summarise the content of the poem. The exam, controlled assessment, or coursework task will focus on specific aspects of the text and will give you a particular question to answer. A common one for coursework, for instance, is 'explore the presentation of love in these poems'. That word 'presentation' is crucial. It means examine the methods the writer uses to discuss or describe love. Summarising the text doesn't answer the question, nor does it focus your essay on presentational devices, such as form or metaphor or rhyme.

Secondly all texts are a network of interconnected meanings. In a poem these connections are intricate and complex. Taking a poem apart to see how it works is like taking the back of an old watch off to explore its cogs, wheels and springs. Something said in line 1 of a poem may link with another thing in line 17. If you take a chronological or sequential approach, working through each stanza, you'll end up repeating yourself. And you'll miss the pattern of how the different parts work together.

Finally a key skill examiners look for is the ability to 'cross-reference', which means making links across a text, seeing how different parts interrelate. It's much easier to cross-reference if each of your paragraphs examines an idea or a technique.

So what should you do instead? You need to break the question down. By exploring how different aspects of the text contribute to the central idea or major overall effect you can approach the questions from different angles. For the question on love you would examine how the writer's use of language (tone, sonic effects or imagery for example) presents love and then how the poem's form and structure contribute to this presentation.

So let's try to apply that thinking to the sample question, 'Explore the ways in which Blake employs language in this poem to create a powerful impact'.

'The Sick Rose'

O Rose thou art sick.

The invisible worm,

That flies in the night

In the howling storm:

Has found out thy bed

Of crimson joy:

And his dark secret love

Does thy life destroy.

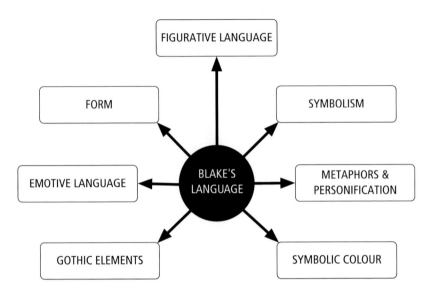

In more detail this looks like:

- **LOTS OF SYMBOLISM** - Using conventional images, such as a 'rose' to symbolise beauty, but in unfamiliar ways - shock effect of first line - series of monosyllables ending with 'sick'. Disturbing sort of love/hate/jealousy poem.

Therefore high density of figurative language - implying a number of different things (depends on what the rose and worm represent - could be man and wife, or England?- perhaps context of French Revolution?) = the effect leaves reader with a sense of mystery.

- **METAPHORS AND PERSONIFICATION** - Eg. the 'howling storm', the 'flying', 'invisible worm'

- **SYMBOLIC USE OF COLOUR** - 'crimson' and sexual imagery - 'worm', 'bed', 'joy', 'love'

- **VIOLENT & EMOTIVE LANGUAGE** - 'O', 'sick', 'howling', 'storm', 'destroy'

- **GOTHIC ELEMENTS** - Darkness and things hidden: 'dark', 'invisible', 'night', 'secret'

- **FORM** - Very short Lyric = condensed = intensity, short lines create forward momentum, hard to stop = sense of inevitability/ fate. The 'rose' cannot escape this fate. Claustrophobic sound world. Rhyme links rose's pleasure with its destruction, implying the one causes the other.

Broadly, in an examination essay you will be expected to make about **FIVE OR SIX STRONG POINTS**. Each point will need to be developed and proven in a paragraph. With an introduction and a conclusion, this would make in total seven or eight paragraphs, which is probably about two and a half sides of writing.

Summary

Instead of writing a sequential essay, or a summary of what happens in the text, focus instead on answering the question set by the examiners. To do this, explore carefully how the different aspects of the text (characters or language for example) contribute to the development of its thematic concerns.

STRUCTURING YOUR ESSAY

This section will deal with four major aspects of the structure of your essays:

1. Sequencing and discourse markers

2. Introductions

3. Conclusions

4. Paragraphing - topic sentences, cohesion and coherence

5. Writing comparative essays

Sequencing

Once you have brainstormed, planned and worked out all the points you wish to make in your essay, your next task will be to put your ideas into the best order. It is worth remembering that when we read material we recall best the first and last sections. This is certainly true for examiners. Therefore it makes sense that after your introduction you start with one of your strongest points.

Imagine you had thought of six points in response to an exam essay question. Points 1, 2, 3, 4, 5 & 6 are in that order because this is the order in which you thought of them. They might, however, be better re-ordered into 3, 5, 1, 4, 6, 2. This is because they make more sense this way, with 3 leading on more easily to 5 than to 4, and because 3 and 2 are your best points and you want to start and end your essay strongly. A concrete example might help.

On our sample 'Of Mice and Men' question, we came up with a number of points regarding the contribution of various key aspects, such as structure, to the presentation of loneliness. Probably our strongest point is about Steinbeck's use of characters to explore the experience, so it would make sense to start our first paragraph after the introduction with a focus on character and characterisaton.

So our essay plan might look something like this:

- **INTRODUCTION**

- **PARAGRAPH 1** - The lonely characters, Curley's wife, Crooks and Candy and how Steinbeck makes us sympathise with their plight (eg shooting of Candy's dog)

- **PARAGRAPH 2** - The causes of their loneliness - prejudice and poverty - the attitudes of other characters. (link to the attitudes of the time and place, ie context)

- **PARAGRAPH 3** - The settings and contexts: The Great Depression 1930's, California, Soledad, the ranch.

- **PARAGRAPH 4** - The language of the novel

- **PARAGRAPH 5** - The contrast to loneliness - the companionship of Lennie and George (strong point to finish with)

- **PARAGRAPH 6** - The narration and Steinbeck's desire for readers to care about these people and to teach us important moral lessons.

- **CONCLUSION**

There is a very handy and easy-to-use tool to help you connect your paragraphs together. This useful tool is called a discourse marker.

Discourse Markers

These are small function words which help you to structure your essay. They are like the signposts on a road indicating the direction your work is taking. There is a number of different types of discourse markers which are determined by the type of text you are writing. If you were writing a narrative story, for example, you would use discourse markers related to time, such as 'before', 'after', 'later', earlier', 'when', 'then'.

We have already established that these temporal discourse markers are not suitable for analytical Literature essays. Instead you can use either of the following:

TYPE	EXAMPLE
Enumeration (this means using a number sequence)	Firstly, secondly, thirdly, fourthly, finally, lastly, in conclusion
Logical argument	If, thus, hence, therefore, moreover, furthermore, however, nevertheless, so

For comparative essays you should employ comparative discourse markers, such as 'similarly', 'in contrast to', 'on the other hand', 'unlike', 'likewise', 'in the same way', 'conversely'.

Introductions

What do you think are the crucial features of a good introduction? Try listing these before you read the next section.

A poor introduction:

- Will be very short, or very long.

- Will tend to take a narrative approach to the task.

- Will give little or no sense of how the question will be answered.

A good introduction:

- Provides an overview of the nature of the text, what it is about and the context in which it was written.

- Succinctly outlines a line of argument that answers the question and indicates how the argument will be developed in the essay. (Sometimes this is called setting an agenda, establishing a hypothesis, or a thesis statement.)

We will use the same essay questions as before on 'Of Mice and Men', 'An Inspector Calls' and 'The Sick Rose':

1. *Explore the significance of loneliness in Steinbeck's 'Of Mice and Men'*

2. *Examine the significance of the role of Eva Smith in Priestley's 'An Inspector Calls'*

3. *Explore the ways in which Blake employs language in his*

poem to create a powerful impact

Compare the following three introductions, rate them out of ten, and decide which one is the best:

▸ **Introductions to essays exploring the theme of loneliness in 'Of Mice and Men'**

1. 'Of Mice and Men' is a novel written by the novelist John Steinbeck. It is about two men, George and Lennie, who go from farm to farm in search of work. At each farm Lennie gets into trouble, mainly because he is so strong but also not very bright. At the ranch where most of the novel is set Lennie first kills a dog and then Curley's wife, which means that George and Lennie are not able to buy a ranch for themselves and 'live off the fatta the lan'. George and Lennie are friends, unlike most of the other characters.

2. 'Of Mice and Men' was written after the Wall Street Crash in 1929. It is set during the Great Depression which followed in the 1930's when many Americans were out of work and vast numbers travelled across the country seeking employment. Some Americans were so poor that they lived in tents or shacks in vast camps. It is known that Steinbeck visited these camps and was warned off writing about the poor by some of the big employers in California. In these sorts of conditions it is not surprising that many people were lonely.

3. 'Of Mice and Men' is a protest novel set in the Great Depression of the 1930's. Sometimes lyrical, sometimes brutal, Steinbeck's

novel explores universal themes such as the power of dreams and the cruelty of prejudice. In the harsh setting of the novel one of the most important of these themes is loneliness. Steinbeck dramatizes how the poverty caused by the Great Depression could grind the compassion out of people, leaving them isolated from each other, bitter and lonely. The experience of loneliness is explored through the language, settings and structure of the novel, but the most important device Steinbeck uses is character and characterisation.

Now try an introduction yourself. On a piece of paper write down why you think this third example is better than the others. Make sure you use the Assessment Objectives to guide you. Then you can turn over the pages and see what our expert said.

What our expert says…

Though the candidate shows some knowledge of the events and characters of the novel in the first example the understanding is at a fairly basic level. Most importantly there is little or no sense of the ideas the novel explores.

The second example is better; the candidate obviously knows quite a bit about the socio-historical context in which the novel was written. However context is only worth marks when it is related directly to the question, when it is used to help explain the significance of the text. In this example it seems to have been shoved in at the start and could have been just as easily shoved into an essay on any question. Here it's only in the last sentence that we actually know what question is being answered. This student has probably used a writing frame.

The third example applies the context directly to the question. It also indicates the genre and style of the novel and some of the other major themes. The question of loneliness is clearly addressed and the candidate indicates the ground they will cover in the essay. More importantly they also suggest what they believe to be the most significant aspect of this novel for this question, on which they are going to focus; character and characterisation.

Compare the following three introductions, rate them out of ten, and decide which one is the best:

▸ **Introductions to essays exploring the significance of Eva Smith in 'An Inspector Calls'**

1. Though she never appears on stage Eva Smith is a significant, perhaps the most significant character in Priestley's didactic detective play, 'An Inspector Calls'. Through their treatment of her, each of the other character's true nature is revealed and the theme of responsibility for others explored. Moreover Priestley was writing just after the Second World War and he wanted his play to encourage British society to pull together. His depiction of the suffering of Eva Smith and others' response to it is a powerful tool for making the audience feel sympathy for the working class.

2. 'An Inspector Calls' is a novel about a woman called Eva Smith who commits suicide after being treated badly by every other character in the play, except the Inspector. The Inspector asks each character questions about their involvement in the Eva Smith case. At the start each character denies being involved,

but the Inspector manages to break through their defences to reveal the truth.

3. A failed politician, J.B. Priestley wrote 'An Inspector Calls' as a play to portray his socialist ideas to a wide audience. He was against the class system, disliked individualism and hated the great imbalance in wealth in the country. He uses the play to get across these political views in an exciting 'whodunit' format. He wrote the play in 1945, in the aftermath of World War II, but he set it in 1912. This allowed the use of hindsight and thus, he could make successful use of dramatic irony.

Clearly the first example is better than the second. Whereas the second piece is a narrative summary, the first piece focuses on the question and suggests a number of ways in which it is going to be answered. As with the best 'Of Mice and Men' introductions, the socio-historical context is used effectively in the first extract. It's important that you notice too that the first example makes clear that 'An Inspector Calls' is a PLAY, whereas the second candidate confuses it with a NOVEL. As these two types of Literature are very different, this is a major, but common, category error. Make sure, in your writing about plays, you refer to some of the following: audience, stage set or stage directions, lighting, props, costume and actors.

The third example is from an essay awarded A* in a GCSE Literature examination. What are the strengths and weaknesses of this introduction? Have a go at listing these before you turn to the next page.

Strengths

✓ Well-written, accurate and fluent

✓ Shows knowledge of genre

✓ Shows understanding of the author's political beliefs and their relevance to the play

✓ States the historical context

✓ Understands how setting the play in the past allowed Priestley to create dramatic irony, a key dramatic device in 'An Inspector Calls'

Weaknesses

✗ What is the question? Feels a bit pre-prepared

✗ The context isn't used to help answer the question

✗ The introduction doesn't establish a thesis statement or line of argument

This goes to show that your writing does not have to be perfect to be awarded a top grade in the examination.

Attempt your own comparative exercise with the following two introductions on 'The Sick Rose'. Once you've completed this task you should have a clear idea of what constitutes a really good introduction.

▸ **Introductions to a question on the powerful language used in 'The Sick Rose'**

1. I think Blake's poem the 'Sick Rose' is about a flower that looks beautiful from the outside but inside it is really 'sick'. Blake says that during the night the flower is attacked by a worm which is 'invisible'. Then there is a storm and the worm finds the rose's

bed and its 'secret' love is then said to 'destroy' the love, perhaps through killing her or it. The poem is a pre twentieth century poem which explains the old english language used.

2. In 'The Sick Rose' Blake creates a mysterious parable in which seemingly feminised concepts of love and beauty are destroyed by dark hidden, seemingly male, forces. The densely symbolic language of the poem creates an intense, claustrophobic world, and the almost hypnotic effect of the poem is heightened by its compactness. Written during the French Revolution in the 1790's the emotional intensity of the poem seems to reflect the violent turmoil in society. The relation of what seems at first to be a perverse love poem to the historical context is not, however, immediately clear to the reader.

Now, before you read on, write down your comments about paragraphs 1 and 2. Make sure you use the marking criteria. Once you've done that you can compare your thoughts with the comments of our expert.

Our expert says...

The second example is better than the first, don't you think? Though in the first one the candidate has got the idea that the poem might be about the difference between appearance and reality - the rose looks healthy but is being eaten away from the inside - this thematic insight is not really developed. Instead we are taken through a summary of the story of the poem.

There is an attempt to put the poem into some sort of historical context. However this context is so broad and undiscriminating that it is virtually meaningless. Thousands and thousands of poems were written before the twentieth century over a period of about seven hundred years. A poem written in 1378 is not likely to have much in common with one written in 1678 or 1878!

The historical context also seems to have been stuck on the end of the introduction as an afterthought. It would be much better employed to help explain the poem. Old English is also a rather imprecise term. In Universities Old English means Anglo-Saxon literature written before the Norman Conquest in 1066! This poem was written in the 1790s, so Old English is pretty wide of the mark.

The second example is very strong. Key ideas are succinctly established. Good points about form and style are supported by relating the text to its historical content.

Conclusions

How do you make your conclusions effective and how do you avoid just repeating your introduction?

If you started your essay with a brief provisional answer, or a hypothesis, you can avoid falling into the trap of writing a conclusion which merely repeats the introduction. In the main body of your essay you will have explored the details of the text as a means of examining the extent to which your provisional answer was correct. In your conclusion you can refine your answer in the light of what you have discovered, or you can confidently conclude that your provisional answer has now been proven to be correct.

Finishing your essay with a telling quotation is sometimes recommended as a way to end strongly. This can work, but make sure you choose a quotation that you didn't need to analyse closely.

The following extract is the conclusion to an examination essay on the presentation of love in Jane Austen's novel, 'Pride and Prejudice'. Read it through and see if you can identify why this is an effective end to the essay. (The entire essay is included in section 5 of this book.)

In conclusion, in a novel in which the characters experience greatly varying degrees of happiness, Jane Austen makes it clear that love is an important factor in determining the strength of affection for one's partner. Love, in the view of Lizzie and the narrator, is also very important in determining the happiness of a marriage – many of "Pride and Prejudice"'s least successful marriages are formed from lust, superficial responses to appearances or for economical stability. Most importantly perhaps, it is clear that love comes only as a result of mutual respect and time to find out about one's partner – in this way, Lizzie and Darcy provide the novel's perfect example of a loving couple.

Strengths

- ✓ The key words of 'happiness', 'love' and 'marriage' are used, showing the writer is focusing on the question.

- ✓ The writer distinguishes between what is shown in the novel about happy and unhappy marriages, showing understanding of the significance of the novel's themes.

- ✓ The writer leaves to the end their strongest point, 'Most importantly…' showing they have thought about which points are most significant and finishing strongly.

✓ The writer illustrates this closing point with the best example from the novel.

Paragraphing

Remember that a paragraph is a collection of sentences on a specific subject. It's a good idea to leave a one line gap between your paragraphs so that the examiner can immediately see you are using them. But bear in mind that indenting or leaving a space after a really long sentence does not turn it into a paragraph. In terms of paragraphing, the key skill you need to master to achieve high grades is the use of analytical paragraphs. Analytical paragraphs are ones that begin with a point, or topic sentence, and which then go on to examine how textual evidence supports this point. Writing good analytical paragraphs involves paying close attention to the following three aspects:

1. Topic sentences

2. Strong endings and making connections

3. Cohesion and coherence

▸ Topic Sentences

It is vital that each of the opening sentences to the paragraphs in your essay starts by establishing the point you are going to develop. This type of an opening sentence is called a 'topic sentence'. The rest of your paragraph will examine the textual evidence you are supplying to prove this point and explore this topic. If you start your paragraphs with phrases like 'during chapter two' or 'after the Inspector has left the

Birlings' you know you are going wrong because these sorts of phrases are not points in answer to a question.

Sometimes it is easy to start paragraphs on one topic and accidentally slip on to another different one. Look at the following example.

Interpretation of the symbol of the 'rose' in Blake's poem is crucial to our understanding. The rose could, of course, symbolise beauty, as it conventionally does in love poems. However in our own time roses are worn as emblems of national identity on English rugby shirts, and so perhaps Blake's rose also suggests England. In this reading England is 'sick' as it has become corrupted in some way by a hidden force, represented by the worm. The worm is a potentially phallic image which suggests male power. In Blake's poem this power is definitely destructive and perhaps the poet is suggesting it is a hidden 'secret' invasion of some sort.

Though this isn't a terrible paragraph you will probably have noticed how the topic has slipped from the symbolism of the rose onto the symbolism of the worm. It would be easy to correct this problem. We could either change the topic sentence to something like, 'the symbolism of the poem is key to its interpretation' or we could finish the paragraph on the phrase 'represented by the worm'. This has the advantage of linking neatly to the next paragraph which can then have the topic of the symbolism of the worm.

▸ Ending strongly, making connections

Try to end paragraphs strongly. This can be achieved by bringing the point you have been exploring to a mini-conclusion. A short emphatic statement will give your writing punch and ensure that your point is firmly made. In the example above the paragraph could have ended with something along the lines of 'so, clearly the rose can be interpreted in a number of ways. So too can its adversary, the worm'. Finishing like this also links your paragraphs coherently and signposts for the reader the topic you are going on to explore next.

▸ Cohesion & coherence

Cohesion refers to the connections made between sentences, to the glue that sticks bits of texts together. Cohesion occurs through repetition of individual words or ideas. Coherence is the term used when these links work together to make overall sense.

A text can be cohesive, but not coherent, but it cannot be coherent without being cohesive. As with your paragraphing, paying attention to the quality of the linking of your sentences will improve your writing significantly. Your aim should be to write coherently, to string ideas together in a logical sequence.

Read the following paragraphs and see if you can identify what is wrong with them. Some are incohesive (disconnected fragments), some incoherent (make no sense) and some are both.

1. *This book is about people. I'm having fish for dinner. Juventus are an Italian football team. Charlie is walking down the road so I turn away and shut the door. 'A cup of tea, please'. The square root of minus one? Androids look like humans.*

2. *'Of Mice and Men' is about loneliness. It is a novel by John Steinbeck. The main characters are Lennie and George. It was written in the 1930s and is about prejudice. It is a protest novel and Steinbeck writes mostly in dialogue with a third*

person narrator.

3. *I'm typing on the computer. My computer screen is black. Referees in football matches wear black. So do undertakers. Funerals are not usually much fun. Usually watching a film is more fun. I like films with good plots. My uncle had a garden plot on which he liked to grow carrots. Rabbits like carrots. Rabbits multiply quickly. Unlike these words on my computer screen.*

4. *'Of Mice and Men' is about loneliness. Loneliness is a terrible feeling connected with our deepest fears of abandonment. Other deep fears include fears of being attacked. In the novel Lennie is attacked by Curley and Curley's wife attacks Crooks verbally.*

Paragraph 1 is just random information stuck together without anything to link the sentences. Sentence 1. is therefore in-cohesive and also incoherent.

Paragraph 2 is better. This one is cohesive, as all the sentences are linked through the subject of 'Of Mice and Men'. It isn't coherent writing, however, because the links are rather random and don't focus on any particular aspect. Nor do they build to a logical explanation or make overall sense.

Paragraph 3 is cohesive as each sentence has a link with the one after it. However it doesn't make sense overall, as there is no single idea developed through the sentences. The sentences are only held together very loosely.

Paragraph 4 is closest to coherent, with a couple of sentences focusing on the topic of loneliness. However it seems like it might be going off onto a new topic of fears.

Writing Comparative Essays

All exam boards require candidates to write comparative essays, either in exams, controlled assessment or for coursework. In almost all examination papers this task is based on the comparison of two poems.

There are two fundamental skills in these essays in addition to the ones tested in single text questions:

1. The subtlety with which the two texts are compared and contrasted.

2. The skill with which a comparative approach is maintained throughout the essay.

▸ **Look at the following examples of introductory sentences written about imaginary poems**

Rate the quality of the comparison from 1 = 'Come on, you can do better than that', to 5 = 'Wow, that's really impressive'. Remember, as you don't know the poems you could only go on how sophisticated the comparison appears to be.

a. I think both these poems were written pre-1914 and so their language is pretty much the same. Although the poems are similar in terms of their tone and thematic concerns, on closer examination their imagery is very different. In both poems the imagery is mostly drawn from nature. However in the first poem the imagery is of nature overgrown and spreading fast, whereas in the second poem the natural imagery conveys order and control.

b. These poems are both alike because they are both set out as verse. The first poem has four stanzas and the second one has five. They also have a similar number of lines, though the second one is a bit longer.

c. These poems are similar because they were both written by men and have women characters in them.

d. These poems are similar in terms of genre as they can both be classified as love poems. However the nature of love explored is entirely different.

e. As both these poems were written before the twentieth century they express similar attitudes. At that time women were often seen as second class, as is shown in the poems.

Now total up your score. By our reckoning you should have a score of about 16.

a. To lump together seven hundred years of Literature as if it was almost the same is extremely imprecise and certainly not 'discriminating': a. is worth 1.

b. This is very good. The candidate is examining similarities and differences and is considering how different aspects of the texts relate (tone, theme, imagery): b. is worth 5.

c. Is not very good. Obviously poems are set out like verse. This is like saying this poem is similar to this poem because they're both poems. However the candidate is trying to comment on differences as well as similarities. It is worth 2.

d. A fairly basic point perhaps, but not immediately obvious and this might open up an interesting line of argument. Perhaps 3 (We're feeling generous).

e. Good. Again differences as well as similarities are noticed. 4 points.

f. Same as the first one. A huge inaccurate generalisation. But they do identify a shared concern of the texts: worth 1 or perhaps 2.

Summary

Make sure you examine differences as well as similarities. Avoid sweeping generalisations. Drill down into the detail. You will pick up high marks if you explore details which initially look like similarities or differences, but which on closer inspection turn out to be the opposite. For example, the imagery is similar in certain ways, but different in others.

▸ **There is a number of ways that a comparative poetry question can be structured.**

The main aspects you should be focusing on, however, are the themes (what the texts are about), what perspective they are written from (narration, or voice) the poet's use of language (which includes sonic effects, tone and imagery) and form and structure (which includes rhyme scheme, stanza form and metre).

Broadly speaking you will need to write one paragraph on each of these aspects for each poem.

STRUCTURE 1	STRUCTURE 2	STRUCTURE 3
Introduction	Introduction	Introduction
Themes in text A	Themes in text A	Themes in text A & B
Voice or narration in text A	Themes in text B	Voice or narration in text A & B
Language in text A	Voice in text A	Language in text A & B
Form & structure in text A	Voice in text B	Form & structure in text A & B
Themes in text B	Language in text A	Conclusion
Voice or narration in text B	Language in text B	
Language in text B	Form & structure in text A	
Form & structure in text B	Form & structure in text B	
Conclusion	Conclusion	

The problem with following structure 1 is that all the comparison has to happen in the second half of the essay. It is therefore very hard to score good A03 marks using this model. Really structure 1 encourages two mini-essays, each focused on a different poem. Therefore we strongly recommend you do not adopt this structure.

Structure 2 will work well, as long as candidates employ comparative discourse markers to make links between the paragraphs on each aspect of the two poems. It also has the benefit of being fairly simple to use. If you are aiming for grades C-A we recommend you use this structure. Structure 3 requires candidates to constantly compare the two texts. It is therefore a more demanding structure, but it could potentially help you to score higher A03 marks. If you are aiming for an A or A* you should practice using this more advanced essay structure. For this structure you will probably need two paragraphs to explore each aspect.

Summary

Try to connect your sentences and your paragraphs through the development of ideas. If you can do this your writing will be coherent and convincing.

Writing essays

It's been quite a long but hopefully not entirely uninteresting journey so far. Now we arrive at the real heart of the matter, the business of actually writing essays. We'll examine essay writing under the following three headings:

1. Using evidence: The analytical paragraph.

2. Writing style: Academic formal style.

3. Proof-reading: Spelling, punctuation, grammar and sense.

USING TEXTUAL EVIDENCE (OR 'QUOTATIONS AND WHAT TO DO WITH THEM')

Use of evidence will be explored under three headings:

1. Quality of evidence.

2. Using key words.

3. Embedding, or integrating, quotations.

Quality of evidence

How, and how effectively, you use textual evidence is probably the most important aspect of your Literature essays, the essential element that more than any other will determine your grade. Fortunately there is a clear scale on which you can place how successfully you are using evidence.

Approximate grade and key qualities of candidates' work

- D - Candidates **IDENTIFY** or **DESCRIBE** some textual details

- C - Candidates **COMMENT** on some textual details

- B - Candidates **DISCUSS** a range of well chosen textual details

- A - Candidates **ANALYSE** a good range of significant textual details

- A* - Candidates **SUSTAIN DETAILED CRITICAL ANALYSIS** of the most significant textual details

How does this look in practice? Well, we'll use Blake's short poem, 'The Sick Rose' to exemplify how you can move up the ladder from D to A*.

Pupils are sometimes tempted to merely describe:

> *In this poem Blake tells us that a specific flower is sick. He goes on to say that it is sick because of the actions of a worm. The worm comes out of the night and a storm and when it discovers the flower bed it destroys the rose. The poem is short, being only eight lines long.*

A little better, but not much, is the identification of features. We'll concentrate on analysing the first line of the poem for all the following examples. The first line is 'O rose thou are sick'.

▸ **D grade**

Blake uses a metaphor in the first line of the poem to compare the rose to something that is sick.

The candidate has correctly identified the technique (metaphor) and its function of comparison.

▸ **C grade**

Blake uses a metaphor in the first line of the poem, comparing a rose to a person or animal that is ill. The sickness suggests that there is something wrong with the rose and that this might be serious.

▸ **B grade**

Building on the previous example, the C grade answer comments on the use of the metaphor and its possible implications.

Blake uses a surprising metaphor, implying that the rose is alive and unwell in some at present unclear way. The word 'sick' is stronger than 'ill' and could relate to either mental or physical illness, or both. It could also suggest a moral sickness, like the phrase 'sick in the head'.

Here the candidate is starting to discuss the significance of the individual words and tease out their effect. So this is a B grade answer.

Blake uses a surprising metaphor in the first line for a number of related reasons. Firstly he creates shock. The poem starts like a conventional love poem addressed to something conventionally beautiful, 'O rose thou art'. The archaic pronoun 'thou' and verb form 'art' emphasise a timeless and traditional approach. The sudden blunt word 'sick' completely changes the tone and how we understand the line. Ideas of beauty are replaced with thoughts of illness and perhaps corruption. A theme of corruption is also suggested by the 'worm' hidden inside the rose.

In a really good response, the candidate will comment on how the writer uses language and the impact this has on the meaning of what they write. In other words they respond to 'how' as well as 'what' the writer has written. The candidate is now exploring the specific language choices in sustained detail, while also considering the effect on the reader, the genre of text and the writer's possible purposes. This is A grade quality work. An A* response would do everything in the example above, sustaining this quality over the whole essay. Ideally it would also show some originality and flair.

You will have noticed in the last example that more of the textual detail, here the language, is put under the microscope of close reading. Another feature of the A grade response is the connection of the first line to an image that comes later in the poem. This is what is meant by 'cross-referencing'.

Employing cross-referencing is another way to raise your marks. Instead of working through individual details of a text, try to see the text as a network of interrelated features. If you find an image of beauty in the first line, try to connect this to another image later in the poem, then examine these two together.

Using key words

When you are quoting from a text it is far better to keep your quotations short and to the point. In most circumstances a good rule of thumb is that quotations should not be longer than two lines.

It is usually unnecessary to write the whole of a quotation in full. Look at the following example and identify how the candidate's use of quotation could be improved.

Blake's choice of colour symbolism makes both the rose and the worm seem morally suspect: '...found out thy bed of crimson joy and his dark secret love does thy life destroy.'

Firstly by getting rid of the line divisions the candidate has indicated that they are unaware of the significance of a key feature of poems. They should either have set the poem out as it would appear on the page:

Blake's choice of colour symbolism makes both the rose and the worm seem morally suspect:

'Has found out thy bed

of crimson joy

and his dark secret love

does thy life destroy'

Or they should have used the convention of oblique slashes (/) to indicate line breaks:

> Blake's choice of colour symbolism makes both the rose and the worm seem morally suspect: 'Has found out thy bed/ of crimson joy/ and his dark secret love/ does thy life destroy'.

Secondly and more importantly, they've quoted half the poem when really they are focusing on just a couple of words. The other words around these are not being examined under the heading of 'colour symbolism' and are therefore irrelevant and should be cut. Far better to write something like:

> Blake's choice of colour symbolism makes both the rose and the worm seem morally suspect. The rose is described as 'crimson' a dark, deep, sensual red and the worm's love is also 'dark'. Like redness, the colour 'crimson' can symbolise a number of related ideas.

In this example the keywords on which the candidate is focusing are embedded within the sentence.

Embedding or integrating quotations

How do you use quotations?

A common way is to make a statement, or point, and then to look for a single quotation to back this up. In good essays the quotation is then examined in some detail.

For example, Blake personifies the weather: 'the invisible worm that flies in the night/ in the howling storm'. By doing this he makes it seem like the whole world is disturbed by the actions of the rose and the worm.

As we established in the section on using key words, it is better to extract and use only the substantive (most important) keywords from a quotation. We hope you'd agree that in the example the most important phrase is 'howling storm'. The rest of the quotation does not contribute to the point we are making. As in the example about colour symbolism the rest of the quotation is redundant and should therefore be cut.

'Embedding' or 'integrating' a quotation meanings placing it within a sentence rather than sticking it at the end of one. To do this successfully the sentence should still make sense if you removed the quotation marks.

For example, the following doesn't quite make sense: Blake personifies the weather 'howling storm', which makes it seem like the whole world is disturbed by the actions of the rose and the worm.

A little rewriting is necessary to arrive at, "Blake personifies the weather as a 'howling storm'", which makes it seem like the whole world is disturbed by the actions of the rose and worm".

In addition to being more stylish, embedding the key words of a quotation makes us focus more on these keywords, makes us notice them more. So we might now comment on the adjective 'howling', which may call to mind wolves or someone crying out in pain, protest or misery. There is also more time and space in the paragraph for us to use more than one quotation, to do some **CROSS-REFERENCING** as we keep emphasising (examiners credit this highly). So we could link 'the howling storm' to the personification of the 'rose' and the 'worm', or to other words that generate the intense, emotional, almost Gothic atmosphere of the poem, such as 'sick', 'worm', 'night', 'dark', 'hidden' and 'destroy'.

"Blake creates an intense, almost Gothic, atmosphere of extreme disturbed emotions and violent action. He personifies the weather as 'howling', as if the whole world of the poem is protesting or crying out in pain. The 'storm' itself suggests violent emotional conditions suitable for such a destructive scene. A further Gothic and mysterious quality is generated through the sense of moral darkness (the adjective 'dark' is repeated twice and the poem is set at 'night') and moral illness (through references to inner corruption). Darkness also obscures what is happening, an idea that is suggested through the adjective 'hidden'".

When you're writing Literature essays it is useful to think of yourself as being like a lawyer in court whose task it is to use evidence to prove your case to a sceptical jury. Or if you prefer, think of yourself as a scientist, testing a hypothesis about a text. To test a hypothesis thoroughly scientists have to examine their data systematically. For students of Literature the data is the words in the text.

WRITING STYLE

We are going to explore writing style under the following five headings:

- Academic Formal Style

- First person vs. depersonalised voice

- Word power - using impressive words

- Controlling sentences

- Using the correct terminology.

Academic formal style

Imagine you have an interview for a job you really want. How do you dress? If you're sensible you will, of course, dress smartly. Turning up to a formal interview dressed casually in your old beach shorts, some flip flops and a pair of sunglasses would probably not be very helpful.

Formal writing style is the equivalent of dressing smartly. To write formally means not using slang or other forms of non-standard English. It means not abbreviating, not using colloquialisms or txt speech. Often in life we adapt the language we use to the situation we're in. The better we can do this usually the more successful we are going to be. Think of the language you use with your friends, or that you might use to a baby, or to a pet. If you used this language to a judge or a policeman you might find yourself in trouble: 'Who's a lovely lickle policeman, then, who's a lovely lickle boy. Yes, you are....yes you are....'

For a GCSE English Literature essay you need to use the right language -

formal, academic style.

Have a look at this example of inappropriate style.

> *At the end of the day in 'OMoM' Lennie's like mentally retarded and this kind of makes him vulnerable to being dissed by other people even though it's not like his fault or nothing.*

There's nothing wrong with the content of this sentence; the problem is the way it has been casually expressed. The candidate needs to distinguish between talking about a text to friends and writing about it in an essay aimed at teachers and examiners.

To summarise, in formal essays you should avoid:

- Using slang

- Abbreviating words

- Using txt speech

- Using colloquialisms

- Using non-Standard English.

First person vs. depersonalised voice

Though there is no hard and fast rule about whether you should use first person or depersonalised voice in English Literature essays, it is generally considered better style to keep mainly to depersonalised voice. The effect of this is to make your writing sound both more formal and more authoritative. It also has the advantage of reserving your use of first person so that you only use it when you want to emphasise your own interpretation or feelings. Some examination boards require you to write about how reading the literature has affected you personally. If you take Cambridge IGCSE, for example, somewhere in your poetry essay you should write a sentence beginning with 'To me this poem is...' and then outline whatever impact you feel the poem has had.

Overuse of the first person, "I", makes writing sound too subjective and unsophisticated, even a little naive. We have used the analogy of a science investigation before. Ideally an English Literature essay should combine the objective, careful, scientific analysis of data with something more emotionally literate, lively and persuasive.

Read the following example. Forget about the content. What impression does the writing create? How would you describe the style?

> *I believe this poem was written in the early 1960's and I think that it is about the theme of treating people unfairly, a theme that was very important at that time. I think this as the writer has used words like 'black' and 'white' with the black being those who are badly treated. I believe the writer is trying to make us not accept bad treatment of people. I think he does this well and I believe some of his use of words is very powerful.*

Before you read our version, try re-writing the above paragraph, improving the writer's style.

> *Written in the early 1960's, this poem tackles the contemporary issue of oppression. In particular the poet uses colour symbolism, specifically 'white' and 'black', in an attempt to persuade the reader to reject prejudice and exploitation. I think the poet's imagery is poignant and powerful, making this a very effective poem.*

You will probably have noticed that we made some other changes to the introduction. Though we did not change the meaning, we substituted more complex words for the ones the candidate used. What is the effect of these changes?

Word power - using impressive vocabulary

Of course you shouldn't use long words and complex vocabulary just for their own sake. That would be a form of dressing up your writing to make it appear more sophisticated than it really is. Always go for clarity of expression over using some fancy terms. However, the vocabulary you employ demonstrates the range of the language you have at your disposal.

And, frankly, sophisticated words can help you to impress the examiners. By sophisticated words we are partly referring to the sort of technical vocabulary, such as metaphor or narration, which we will go on to explore in the next few pages of this book. But we also mean words that have a number of syllables and that are derived from Latin and Greek. Words that can actually save you time when they are used precisely.

For example, look at how we changed some of the vocabulary in the model essay samples used in this book.

ORIGINAL TEXT	EDITED VERSION
Treating people unfairly	Oppression
At that time	Contemporary
Used words	Uses colour symbolism
Who are badly treated	Prejudice
Trying to make us not accept	An attempt to persuade
Bad treatment	Exploitation
His use of words	The poet's imagery
Powerful	Poignant and powerful

Winston Churchill famously apologised for writing a long letter because he didn't have the time to write a shorter one. What did he mean by this? He meant that sometimes it takes more time to really think about what we want to say and to express this succinctly. A master with language, Churchill also understood the power of using the right words as precisely as a surgeon uses a scalpel.

Controlling sentences

When we are writing very quickly under great pressure, as when we are writing under examination conditions, it is really easy for any one of us, however good we usually are at writing, to lose a bit of control of our syntax (word order) and our punctuation so that our writing tends to become imprecise and sentences are going on forever and end up being far too long so that we almost forget at the end of them what we started off by saying. The reader ends up with too little real sense of what we were trying to communicate. As, hopefully, we've just demonstrated.

Have a look at some of your own Literature essays. Check to see if you write very long sentences. Practise writing shorter, punchier sentences. Use the rule of thumb that each sentence should deal with one idea. If you move on to a new idea start a new sentence. In time you should find that your writing will become much clearer.

Another problem that can arise if you write overlong sentences is a loss of control over clauses. Look at this example from an 'A' level essay on the poetry of W.B. Yeats:

> *In this poem, written by Yeats at the start of the twentieth century, in response to both personal and political events, Yeats, who was an Irish writer from an Anglo-Irish background, uses a number of familiar images.*

You can now attempt to re-write this sentence so that it is less cluttered and clumsy.

Clearly this student has tried to pack too many ideas into one sentence. But if they did want a long sentence they could substantially improve it simply by keeping the noun and verb much closer together.

For example,

> *Written at the start of the twentieth century by the Anglo-Irish poet Yeats in response to both personal and political events, this poem uses a number of familiar images.*

Better though would be,

> *Written at the start of the twentieth century by the Anglo-Irish poet, Yeats, this poem uses a number of familiar images. The*

poem was written in response to events which had both a
personal and political significance for the poet.

Using the correct technical terminology

All GCSE subjects have their own technical terminology. Think of all the different words and phrases used in Mathematics, for instance: vectors, differentiation, quadratic equations, square roots, adding up and so forth. It is essential that in a GCSE Literature essay you use the technical terminology confidently. Not only will you be rewarded for this in terms of marks for writing, using technical vocabulary will make you focus on a writer's techniques.

It is also a more economical and exact way of writing. Look, for example, at the following:

> *The poet compares one thing physical, a 'rose', with something*
> *else, perhaps an idea such as beauty or love, by saying it is 'sick'.*

That could be clearer:

> *The poet uses symbolism so that a physical 'rose' suggests ideas,*
> *such as beauty or love. It is the personification of the 'rose' as*
> *'sick' which makes this metaphorical quality of the flower*
> *apparent to the reader.*

You will find a list of the most important technical terms for novels, plays and poems in the next section. Make sure you know what these mean and try to include a good number in your essays.

Summary

Check the length of your sentences. Use one sentence per idea. Keep your subject and verb as close together as possible. Use the correct technical vocabulary. Instead of using the first person, 'I think that', use the more authoritative depersonalised voice. And try to include some sophisticated words.

PROOFREADING: SPELLING, PUNCTUATION, GRAMMAR AND SENSE

All exam boards reserve some marks for the technical accuracy of candidates' writing. Moreover, writing accurately will mean that you communicate more clearly. It is essential that you proofread your work before submitting it. In an examination, leave yourself about five minutes per essay to proofread properly.

Re-read a few essays you have written. Look for words that you often misspell. Set about eradicating these spellings. For GCSE Literature there is a set of key technical terms. Make sure that you use a good range of these in your essays and that you know how to spell each one of the following:

- Narration/ narrator
- Omniscient narration
- Characters
- Metaphor
- Imagery
- Stanza
- Caesura
- Metre
- Simile
- Onomatopeia
- Personification
- Scene

- Playwright
- Tragedy
- Soliloquy
- Monologue
- Protagonist
- Enjambment
- Adjective
- Pentameter
- Dramatic irony
- Stage
- Set
- Costume
- Props

As an examiner, it is usually possible to accurately predict a candidate's grade just from the range of punctuation they use. Candidates who only accurately use full stops and commas are often D grade. Candidates who accurately use semi-colons are invariably A*s. Therefore it makes sense to ensure that you use at least a few different types of punctuation in your essay.

Remember punctuation wasn't dreamt up by English teachers in order to torture pupils. It is an essential device to help make writing clear. The most fundamental thing is for you to understand what makes something a sentence.

Look at the following example of poor punctuation and see if you can identify what's wrong:

> *Steinbeck's novel is at times lyrical and at other times brutal. In particular the descriptions of the Californian landscape and of George and Lennie's dream are often richly poetic. Which contrasts with the descriptions of the bunkhouse.*

The problem here is the last section; "which contrasts with the descriptions of the bunkhouse" is a sentence fragment not a sentence. You can tell it isn't a proper sentence because it does not make sense standing on its own. All sentences need at least a subject and a verb. This fragment does not have a subject.

Another common, similar error is when candidates use the conjunction 'whereas' at the start of a sentence.

> *Mr Birling does not care about what happened to Eva Smith, he is only concerned with maintaining his own reputation. Whereas Sheila is more concerned with her own faults and errors.*

Extract the last section and isolate it and it becomes clear that it is not a complete sentence: "whereas Sheila is more concerned with her own faults and errors". Like the other example it needs a subject. Instead of a full stop after 'reputation', a comma could be used.

Proofread the following and identify the mistakes: One point for a punctuation error and inaccurate use of capitals, two for a spelling, three for a grammatical mistake.

> *of Mice and Men is a book, by steinbeck which is about two freinds who travel around together. One of them, Lennie, is a big*

and metally subnormal. The other george is small and quick thinking. They share a dream. Which is of owning there own ranch and 'livin' offa the fatta of the lan' many other charcters share this dream Candy who's dog is killed is the first to become involved. Then Crooks the black stable buck is drawn in however Carlson never gets drawn in because like lots of the other characters he's a mean spirited loner that feels no compassion for anyone.

Total score: 27

Before we go on to examine how you should tackle an unseen poetry question, let's examine a complete essay in some detail. The following essay was written in GCSE examination conditions and explores the significance of isolation as a theme in 'Of Mice and Men'.

At the end of each section of the essay we will see that we've added examiner style comments to highlight the particular strengths of this response.

Steinbeck's 'Of Mice and Men' is a protest novel set in the early 1930's, during the Great Depression. Geographically, it is set in California, where the economic strife had left many migrant workers desperate for work to allow them to survive. Migrant workers travelled between ranches, looking for jobs. They were at the mercy of the ranch owners and were competing against each other in a fight for survival. Our two central characters, George and Lennie, are two such workers.

<u>Comments</u>

✓ This is an effective opening, establishing the type of novel

✓ It also demonstrates understanding of how the socio-historical setting affected people

There is a key difference however, between George and Lennie and the other workers: they have companionship in each other, whereas other workers are lonely and isolated. It is partly this fear of isolation that keeps George and Lennie together.

We meet other characters on the ranch who do not have this companionship, though some crave it. For example, when Whit finds a letter from a worker he once knew in a magazine, he "cries" out with excitement, because this shows there is something outside the tedious, isolated life he lives. He clings onto this thought.

<u>Comments</u>

✓ The candidate supports their point about how George and Lennie are different.

✓ The quotation is neatly embedded and the language is commented on.

Isolation has hardened many characters and made them selfish and mistrustful. For example, Curley, an "angry little man", is resentful of the way his wife talks to the workers; he is insecure, so he backs himself up with threats of violence: "No big son-of-a-

bitch is gonna laugh at me!"

His wife is known only as "Curley's wife", depersonalising her and taking away her sense of a separate identity. Very aptly she displays the effects of isolation on a person. She is the only woman on the ranch and Curley is fiercely protective of her. The ranch workers try to avoid her for fear of repercussions. Hence, she has no-one to talk to, to confide in. Her days are lonely, so she craves attention and companionship: "I get lonely", "I can't talk to nobody but Curley" .

Comments

✓ Further examples of the impact of isolation are established.

✓ Again there is brief and useful comment on language.

Isolation makes her resentful of others. For example, when she speaks to Crooks, Candy and Lennie in Crooks' room, she dismissively calls them "bindle stiffs" even though she is enjoying their company. Then she whips round on Crooks, telling him "Nigger, I could get you strung up on a tree so easy it ain't even funny". This is an extremely brutal remark that she uses to defend herself; isolation makes people suspicious and defensive, and this is demonstrated by numerous characters in the novel, Curley and his wife in particular.

Crooks, however, is surely the most isolated character in the novel. As a black man, he is treated as inferior, kept in a room by the stables like an animal, with a 'cot' full of hay instead of a proper bed. Nobody wants to be friends with a 'nigger', so he is segregated. We can see the long term resentment this sustained isolation has brought about. "This here's my room. Nobody got any right in here but me". As his battered book of law shows, he is clinging on to what few rights he does have.

<u>Comments</u>

✓ The candidate ranges widely across the text finding good evidence to support their ideas.

✓ They show that they are aware of the most significant examples.

Many of the relationships between the characters are built on isolation and a fear of it. The ranch workers are protective of what little they have and everybody is suspicious of one another. Being isolated for so long has taught them not to invest their emotions for fear of losing them; they have been let down too many times. This is most clear in Carlson's line at the end of the novel which contrasts so powerfully with the pity the reader is encouraged to feel over the death of Lennie.

However, George and Lennie are free from this isolation; "we got each other", and this sets them aside. Together they dream of their ranch, where they would work together. Steinbeck almost lets them see success when they get close to their dream farm, but then all is lost when George tragically shoots Lennie.

Isolation plays a vital part in "Of Mice and Men". It creates the atmosphere, it moulds the characters and sets up the events that occur during the novel's course; Curley's wife would not have died if she had not been so desperate for human contact with Lennie. Isolation was inherent in the bitter realities of the lives of migrant workers during the Great Depression and this is shown poignantly in Steinbeck's novel

Comments

- ✓ The essay concludes effectively, with a strong focus on the question.

- ✓ A coherent, logically developed argument is well supported by evidence.

- ✓ Overall this is a good Band 6 essay.

OTHER TYPES OF RESPONSES TO LITERATURE

Tackling the Unseen Poem

For some examination boards, when you are presented with an unseen you will be given printed guidance of the aspects you should focus your analysis on. If you are not given this information you should apply what you know about analysing all literary texts. This will lead you to analysing:

1. What the poem is about.

2. How it's written.

We can refine this further into:

1. Themes

2. Voice or narration

3. Language

4. Form and structure

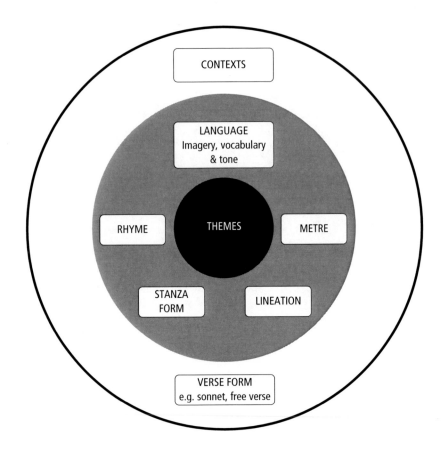

The vital thing for you to remember is to relate the small details of the text, such as the poet's choice of adjectives, to the large scale of its themes. In other words how do the techniques the writer employs contribute to the presentation of his or her ideas?

WJEC is the only board to have a paper on which candidates have to write about two unseen poems. More common is the sort of approach taken by AQA. The following example is taken from a recent AQA GCSE Higher Tier Literature paper.

Read the poem below and answer the question that follows.

▸ **'How to Leave the World that Worships Should'**

Let faxes butter-curl on dusty shelves.

Let junkmail build its castles in the hush

of other people's halls. Let deadlines burst

and flash like glorious fireworks somewhere else.

As hours go softly by, let others curse

the roads where distant drivers queue like sheep.

Let e-mails fly like panicked, tiny birds.

Let phones, unanswered, ring themselves to sleep.

Above, the sky unrolls its telegram*,

immense and wordless, simply understood:

you've made your mark like birdtracks in the sand -

now make the air in your lungs your livelihood.

See how each wave arrives at last to heave

itself upon the beach and vanish. Breathe.

Ros Barber

* 'telegram' – an early form of urgent messaging

EXAM QUESTION: What do you think is the poet's attitude towards the way we live and work in the modern world and how does she present this attitude to the reader?

Try planning an answer to this question before you read our response.

AQA has directed us to examine two aspects, the poet's attitude and how they write.

The first part of the question seems pretty straightforward. All we need to do is look at the items that are repeated often in the poem. This list will give us a good sense of what the poet is concerned about: faxes, junkmail, deadlines, traffic, emails, phone calls. These are everyday features of modern communication, particularly associated with the world of office work. What are these means of communication actually doing in the poem? They're gathering dust on shelves, piling up, being ignored. These are all forms of communication which are not getting through, that are 'unanswered'. Or the poet would like to be able to ignore them all because she sees them as restricting, stressful irritants disrupting her sense of peace.

The annoyingly insistent noisy quality of modern life, as the poet sees it, is emphasised in the last six lines (or sestet) through contrast. The natural landscape suggests freedom, beauty, peace, contemplation, timelessness, true communication and real understanding, all qualities opposite to the world of the faxes and emails.

How does she present this attitude? We've already begun to answer this question. We've identified the fact that Barber uses lists, that she focuses on the idea of communication, or rather the failure to communicate, and that she uses contrast (a more technical term is antithesis). To this list we could add the metaphors "build its castles," "the sky rolls out its telegram" and the series of similes "deadlines burst /and flash like glorious fireworks", "drivers queue like sheep", "emails fly like panicked birds".

It is as if the modern man-made things have developed a will and a life of their own, another way of suggesting that forms of mass communication have got out of control. In contrast the sky is the active agent, with the gentle verb "unrolls" suggesting slowness and ease. If the modern world is claustrophobic, anxious and airless, in the natural landscape the poet can breathe properly.

Another repeated word is the verb let. This suggests we should 'allow' ourselves to free ourselves from the pressures of modern life. It is almost like a prayer or a wish that this wonderful liberating experience could happen when all these pressures can be ignored. In terms of the narration or voice of the poem, there is also a sense of instruction. Grammatically, the first word 'let' is a command (as are 'now make' and the last word 'Breathe'), and we realise the poem is addressed to someone - 'you've made your mark,' 'your lungs'.

The form and structure contribute to the poem's argument. Firstly this is a sonnet, so it is itself a traditional form of communication, a creation of space in contrast to the cluttered noisiness of emails and traffic and faxes and phone calls. Secondly the sonnet is also conventionally used for love, so it seems to be employed ironically here - until we remember that the poem is addressed to an unknown 'you', who, we realise, is the beloved.

We have already noted the structural point that the poem is built on a contrast. The first eight lines (technically called the octave) are packed with the business of modern life; the last six provide a vivid contrast.

They offer an escape, a sanctuary of simple beauty that is timeless - the sky, birdtracks, sand, air, wave, beach - and suggest that this is really where we can properly, profitably, live - "make the air in your lungs your livelihood". Long assonating vowels (where the vowel sounds echo across the sentence) in the last couplet emphasise this sense of release and opening up of experience: See how **ea**ch wave arrives at last to h**ea**ve/ itself upon the b**ea**ch and vanish. B**rea**the.

Summary

Make sure you have a strategy for approaching an unseen question. You might like to read our book, 'Art of Poetry' which outlines a highly successful approach in more detail than is possible here.

Exemplar essays

Finally, we've reached the last stop on our journey. By now you probably want to see what real essays look like and you may be wondering what an A* GCSE Literature examination essay is actually like in the flesh. The following examples are essays which achieved grades from A* to C in English Literature examinations. We've given you a range to look at, with essays on:

1. Wordsworth: 'Upon Westminster Bridge'

2. two poems by Seamus Heaney

3. Priestley: 'An Inspector Calls'

4. Golding: 'Lord of the Flies'

5. Wilde: 'The Importance of Being Earnest'

6. Austen: 'Pride and Prejudice'

Two of the poetry essays are comparative pieces from a few years ago, before there was a requirement to refer to the text's socio-historical context (AO4). The other two poetry essays are on Wordsworth's poem.

We have marked each essay with examiner-style comments so that you can see where the candidates are scoring marks. Also included is an extra bonus essay on 'An Inspector Calls'. We would like you to have a go at playing the examiner by marking it in the same style as we used. Use this partly as a language exercise - to try a different, more formal style of writing which suggests analysis and evaluation. Then you can compare our results. You will certainly learn more from this experience if you stop your journey for a moment or two. Here's a chance to get off the road for a short break and to admire some literary scenery.

So, before moving on to the following essays we encourage you to read through Wordsworth's poem at least a couple of times. Reading it will help you to appreciate the strengths and weaknesses of the sample essays. Both essays are exploring the presentation of London in Wordsworth's 'Upon Westminster Bridge'.

Here once again are the assessment objectives:

- **AO1 -** Respond to texts critically and imaginatively; select and evaluate relevant textual detail to illustrate and support interpretations

- **AO2 -** Explain how language, structure and form contribute to writers' presentation of ideas, themes and settings

- **AO3** - Make comparisons and explain links between texts, evaluating writers' different ways of expressing meaning and achieving effects

- **AO4 -** Relate texts to their social, cultural and historical contexts; explain how texts have been influential and significant to self and other readers in different contexts and at different times

▸ 'Upon Westminster Bridge'

Earth has not anything to show more fair

Dull would he be of soul who could pass by

A sight so touching in its majesty

This city now doth like a garment wear

The beauty of the morning; silent, bare,

Ships, towers, domes, theatres and temples lie

Open unto the fields, and to the sky;

All bright and glittering in the smokeless air.

Never did sun more beautifully steep

In this first splendour valley, rock, or hill;

Ne're saw I, never felt, a calm so deep

The river glideth at his own sweet will:

Dear God! The very houses seem asleep

And all that mighty heart is lying still!

▸ Essay 1 explores Wordsworth's presentation of London

Wordsworth conveys a vivid sence of wonder in this poem. One of the ways he achives this is by using personification. When you give the object, place or thing characteristics or looks of a person it is called personification. The poet employs personification throughout this poem because the city that he keeps returning to is actually a woman of his dreams.

The student understands personification and correctly states that this is a major poetic device used in this poem. The point about how the city represents a woman is rather unclear, but suggests some contextual knowledge.

Wordsworth seems to be totally obsessed with the city/woman. You can tell how much Wordsworth is attracted even by reading the very first line, 'Earth hath not anything to show more fair'. This quote shows the city and the woman are the best as there is nothing better.

Wordsworth is constantly complimentary. For example he used the line, 'a sight so touching in its majesty' By this he is saying that it moves him when he looks at the city as it looks splendid and royal, like a queen.

There is evidence here of some understanding of Wordsworth's feelings. The quotations are well chosen to support the point. Though it is not developed in any detail, there is the beginning of some analysis of the quotations.

'Composed Upon Westminster Bridge' is written as a sonnet and the whole poem rhymes. Every final word of every alternat lines rhymes for example the last word of the line 3 ect. This helps make the poem sound in harmony.

Wordsworth also chooses to use many descriptive words. He does this because he wants to create an image in the reader's mind. He picks words that make us full of wonder at the beauty of the city. He makes the reader wonder by using lines such as 'all bright and glittering in the smokeless air' and 'Ne'er saw I a calm so deep'. These quotes make the city seem peaceful and beautiful. There is an emphasis on light.

Finally Wordsworth says the houses are asleep. 'And all the mighty heart is lying still'. In other words the city has not woken up yet, and nothing is moving. This is why he can have this special moment of thinking.

What mark would you give this essay? Can you explain why?

- **GRADE** - Low 'C'

- The student shows a basically sound understanding and makes a reasonably developed personal response.

- Appropriate evidence is generally used to support the points made. There is some focus on the language and the form, with some response to how these contribute to the poem's meaning.

- There is, however, a number of technical errors and the analysis of quotations could be developed in more detail.

For the second of our sample essays the examiner's comments will come at the end. You should only read these once you have made an attempt at marking the work yourself.

▸ **Essay 2**

Wordsworth's poem communicates a sense of awe and wonder of the view of the city, firstly through the description of the city as if is alive. Even its 'houses seem asleep' which creates to the sense of wonder through the personification. Secondly Wordsworth uses words associated with light and with royalty. Lastly he compares the city and finds it more beautiful than anything else.

He describes this moment as a very delicate one, which suggest wonder, because city's are usually very busy places and at this time London would have been busy. The setting of the morning is also important as this can be a peaceful time, when the city seems suspended in a dream like atmosphere, and we understand this is a personal moment of calm for Wordsworth.

Quietness contributes to the sense of wonder. Wordsworth describes the city as if it is the most beautiful place on the earth; 'Earth has nothing to show more fair', which is an unusual thing to say about a city. Cities are more often described as bad places with fog and smoke, like in Victorian London. In contrast this city is a bright, glittering place. The light also suggests the city might be religious. He also says that only someone very 'dull' could miss this beauty as it is so striking.

The city is also compared to a person wearing a 'garment', so we might think the city is female. The descriptions of bright and glittering makes us think of royalty, so the city is like a Queen which fits the image of the 'heart' at the end of the poem as the queen can be seen to be the heart of the nation.

The calmness is the most important theme of the poem. Even the Thames is calm and 'glideth' at 'his own sweet will'. This quote suggests the river is free and moves easily. This quote is also a personification. The parts of the city becoming things that are living helps generate a sense of awe and wonder.

The poem is composed on Westminster Bridge which is important as this places Wordsworth above the action of the city, looking down on it. He is not in among the people, but looking down on it from a position of superiority. The whole poem doesn't mention any people, which also helps to create a quiet and calm atmosphere.

There are no negative aspects to the city, no flaws. Instead he uses words such as 'majesty' wich also has royal associations. The form of the poem is a sonnet, which is unusual, because this is normally a love poem. So Wordsworth's poem is a sort of love poem to the city of London.

Now it's your turn to be the examiner. What grade would you give this? See if you can use the AOs to explain your reasons. What are this essay's strengths and its weaknesses? When you're ready, you can read on and see if our expert agrees.

✓ This candidate understands how Wordsworth creates his effects with language.

✓ They are able to respond personally to the images in the poem and they are beginning to make insights about the effects of language and form.

✓ Although the Victorian reference is inaccurate, there is still some attempt to apply their knowledge about Wordsworth's context to how the poem is written.

✓ The style is straightforward and clear.

Weaknesses

X The analysis of language is vague and doesn't go into enough detail to achieve a high 'B'.

X Comments on the language in the poem aren't consistently backed up by apposite and pithy quotation from the text.

X The sequencing of points is not very clear or logical. The 'agenda', outlined usefully in the introduction, is not carried through into the body of the essay.

X Some of the phrasing lacks sophistication 'cities...are bad places', the sentence structure is rather repetitive and there is a smattering of spelling errors.

Have a read of Heaney's poems 'Churning Day' and 'An Advancement of

Learning' before you read the essays. These are the last two poems we will ask you to read in this book. Both poems can be found easily through a quick internet search.

▸ **Essay 3 compares 'Churning Day' and 'An Advancement of Learning' by Seamus Heaney.**

Both "Churning Day" and "An Advancement of Learning" are written by Seamus Heaney, a poet who was brought up in rural Ireland.   As a result, a lot of his poetry deals with childhood innocence in contrast with the experiences of growing up.   As he wrote these poems in the 1960's, they both carry an undercurrent of war in reference to the 'Troubles' in Ireland during that time.

The style is succinct and shows a solid grasp of the influence of contexts (AO4)

Firstly, both poems have very similar themes.   <u>They are both written in retrospective, looking back nostalgically at a time gone by using military language – "Bridgehead" and rural –"muddler".</u> <u></u> Another theme is that of transformation: shown in "Churning Day" by the change from <u>"white" milk and butter cream to the "gold flecks" of butter "dancing" in the churn</u> **and in "An Advancement of Learning" by the poet's change in attitude towards his fear of rats, finishing by "crossing the bridge" which is representative of conquering his fear.*

The comparison of the themes of the poems is both careful and intelligent, revealing a mature level of critical awareness (AO3/1)*. Also this candidate is able to discuss language in some depth and has a good eye for detail in the expression of points (AO2)**However the discussion of analysis is not technically in-depth enough to warrant an A*(for example, explaining the effect of the metaphor 'dancing').

Secondly, Heaney has a great fondness for neologism, creating highly effective words that conjure up wonderful mental images: for example in "Churning Day" he uses the word "plumping" to describe the kettles used to sterilise the churn. <u>This effectively describes the round shape of the kettles.</u>* In "An Advancement of Learning" he uses "slimed" to describe the movement of the rat, showing how he feels disgusted by it. It is also surrounded by other slimey-sounding words, such as "slobbered". "Churning Day" also used sound effects, contrasting the long vowels of "cool, porous" with the short vowels of "gland, cud and udder".

The discussion of language remains focussed and shows some insight, backed up with short, relevant quotes (AO2)*. The comparison is sustained and well-balanced (AO3)

Lastly, the use of tone and structure shows how the transformation takes place in the duration of the poem. "Churning Day" has 4 stanzas of 9 or 8 lines, with a half-line in the middle over lines 17 and 18 that cuts the poem in half. It may refer to the slabs of butter, but it creates a significant difference between the first two stanzas which are about the effort put in, and the last two stanzas, which concern the reward and the satisfaction of achievement.

"An Advancement of Learning" has a slightly less noticeable change, but the poem has a loose rhyme scheme of ABAB, but stanza 5 disrupts the rhythm by going ABBA. This relates to the

*poet's sudden change of heart, with the 4 stanzas preceding it
using words like "hunched", "curtly" and "dirty-keeled" to create
a threatened tone, while the 4 stanzas proceeding it use a words
like "clockworked, "raindrop" and "tapered".*

The essay's structure is secured by the clear use of discourse markers to link paragraphs together. The poetic form is looked at with some imagination revealing a well-developed critical awareness of its effect (AO2). Again the discussion of the effects of form are not sophisticated enough to warrant A*, however the analytical focus is secure.

*In conclusion, both poems use themes, language, tone and
structure to vividly describe the poet's experience, creating poems
that catch the reader's attention.*

Comments

✓ **GRADE A**

- ✓ This has a clear and well-structured form, using connectives to link ideas and enable comparison.

- ✓ It maintains its focus on the language of the two poems throughout and the analysis of the effects of words and form is quite well-developed. To get on to the A* this should aim to increase the detail in which language is discussed.

- ✓ The style is clear, often using language critically and with insight to express complex ideas. The spelling and grammar are mostly very accurate.

- ✓ A solid knowledge of context is shown at the start but this isn't exemplified meaningfully in the body of the essay.

▸ **Essay 4 also compares 'An Advancement of Learning' with 'Churning Day'. This essay is a little better than the previous one, meaning that it just creeps in to A*.**

Title:Choose two poems from the Best Words anthology which describe events in a particularly memorable way. Discuss how this is achieved.

'An Advancement of Learning', by Seamus Heaney, is written in first person narrative voice and describes the fears and childhood memories of a man and his meeting with a rat. The scene of the poem is an urban setting in an area adjacent to a river which is described as 'pliable, oil-skinned'. The urban setting is emphasised by words such as 'embankment', 'gables' and 'railing'. The whole surroundings sound as though they are grey, murky and un-clean. This is emphasised, as even the swans are 'dirty-keeled'.

A confident opening, making a few solid points about narrative voice, theme and setting (AO1). The candidate wastes no time in getting into the detail of the poem (AO2). Ideally, however, there would have been some comparison with the second poem (AO3).

In contrast to this, another poem by Heaney, 'Churning Day' is very much set in rural surroundings and pastoral images are evoked by the mention of the churning process and the farmhouse. In contrast, the process is made to seem industrial, as the house is described with an extreme simile: 'acrid as a sulphur mine'. The house is made to appear like a factory, as the scale of the process is commented on; 'the butter in soft printed slabs was piled on the pantry shelves'. Here plosive alliteration is used to for emphasis.

Some good points are established. The candidate notices the contrasts between the poem in settings and imagery (A03). Technical aspects are identified (simile, plosive alliteration) and analysed briefly (A02). A critical interpretation is advanced (A01). Although the candidate's approach is clearly analytical, the analysis could have been closer and more developed.

In a similar way in 'An Advancement of Learning' Heaney uses an extended metaphor of a battle in a war against the rats; 'I established a dreaded Bridgehead', 'he trained on me'. The enemy in the form of a rat is described in a very detailed manner, a process of closer inspection that leads the narrator to realise that the rat is not in fact that terrifying, in fact it is battered and worn; 'the raindrop eye, the old snout'. Heaney uses several techniques to describe the narrator's situation and the fear he is experiencing. One particularly effective description of the horrible rat uses sibilance, onomatopoeic words such as 'slobbered' and 'smudging' are used alongside 'slime' and 'sickened'.

The candidate keeps comparison to the fore, using comparative discourse markers, such as 'similar' and 'likewise' (AO3). They cross-reference effectively (A02) recognising the war metaphor. The candidate prioritises information to focus on Heaney's use of sound effects (A02) showing they are alert to the sound of the poem as well as its meanings.

Likewise Heaney uses several poetic techniques in 'Churning Day'.

For example, he uses enjambment to create an almost uncontrolled, chaotic style. The energetic process of the butter-making is further described by the use of onomatopoeia, as words such as 'plash and gurgle' and 'pat and slap' illustrate. Much of the poem, as shown here, appeals vividly to the reader's senses, particularly the sounds and texture; 'thick-crust, coarse-grained as limestone rough-cast'. These chunky phrases emphasise the tactile nature of the work. Additionally, the drawn out vowels of 'cool, porous earthenware' help to express the long process of churning, which is also incredibly hard work; 'Arms ached. Hands blistered'.

The comparison is sustained (AO3) effectively. More technical terms are used to aid analysis of the writer's technique - onomatopeia, vowel sounds (AO2). Some reference is made to form (enjambment) which is neatly related to overall structural effect.

However, Heaney makes sure that the reader recognises that all this hard work is worthwhile as the transformation of the butter is made to seem like alchemy; 'where finally gold flecks began to dance'. Additionally, these gold flecks are personified, as they 'dance' and are 'fished'.

The candidate moves the interpretation on with a discourse marker of argument (however) (AO1). They perceptively recognise the central metaphor of alchemy and go on to explore the effect of the writer's specific choices of vocabulary (AO2).

All the techniques used in these two poems by Seamus Heaney help to create an extremely descriptive form of poetry that pulls the reader into the scenes of the poem. Both poems dramatise transformations, but whereas 'An Advancement of Learning' explores fear 'Churning Day' evokes something magical.

Comments

✓ The essay concludes by drawing the two poems together to recognise similarities and differences.

✓ Overall, although the close analysis could have been more detailed, this is a discriminating, well considered and well written response in which the candidate successfully sustains a close comparison of the two poems.

✓ A very good appreciation of Heaney's techniques is demonstrated, covering a good range in a short amount of time.

✓ This essay fits best into the bottom of Band 6, grade A*.

English Literature GCSE Marking Criteria
Band 6

✓ Considered/qualified response to task and to the text.

✓ Details linked to interpretation.

✓ Appreciation/consideration of writer's uses of language and/or form and/or structure and effect on readers/audience.

✓ Thoughtful consideration of ideas/themes.

✓ Information is presented in a way which assists with communication of meaning. Syntax and spelling are generally accurate.

▸ **Essay 5 explores the theme of responsibility in 'An Inspector Calls'**

J.B. Priestley wrote 'An Inspector Calls' in 1945, a significant period historically for England. The country was emerging from the devastation of two world wars and people were determined to build a better, more caring society than that of the 1930s, a decade marked by unemployment and economic depression.

The play is set in 1912, a time of huge inequality with rigid gender and class boundaries. This gives the audience hindsight, allowing us to appreciate the irony of Birlings' views, such as that 'nobody wants war' and also encourages a parallel to be drawn between the events of the play and society's failure to learn from the First World War.

In relating to the audience the events surrounding the downfall of the lower class Eva Smith and also each character's attitude to their own part in this tragedy, <u>Priestley makes use of 1912's unequal society to demonstrate that a fair | just society depends on compassion and responsibility for our fellow citizens.</u> * The play raises the question of to what extend Eva's downfall was a result of the society in which she lived, as <u>Priestley uses her to represent the innocence of all people,</u> * which can be destroyed if not given the dignity deserved.

*This has a sophisticated understanding of how context influences Priestley's text, which is made directly relevant to the specific question asked. (AO4) The essay is focussed, clearly answering the question, and the argument is made clear by the end of this paragraph.

This is clearly shown as we learn of the hugely selfish attitudes of some characters towards Eva's situation: Mrs Birling, for example, cannot see how the suicide of a lower class person affects her or her family, as she dismisses people like Eva as 'girls of that class' *and declares that 'she only had herself to blame'.* Similarly, Mrs Birling, refuses to show compassion for Eva as he adopts the attitude that her tragedy was her own fault: 'and then she got herself into trouble there I suppose?' In this way Priestley advocates that 'we are responsible for each other' by portraying Eva as an innocent victim of others' selfishness.

This candidate knows the play well and is able to use apposite and succinct quotes* to illustrate their point. The response is critical and shows real engagement with the wider significance of character (Mrs Birling in this case) (AO1). The depth of understanding is displayed in the discourse marker 'similarly' indicating that the point is going to be explained in more depth.

> *Another way in which Priestley advocates this message is through Inspector Goole, who could be seen as an instrument of justice in the play, persuading the characters to admit their guilt and accept responsibility, thus voicing Priestley's own conscience.**
> *Throughout his interrogations, the Inspector keeps to his principle that 'if you're easy with me, I'm easy with you'. Consequently passing harsh moral judgements on those characters who refuse to see the extent of their own crime. When Birling stubbornly declares that 'I can't take any responsibility' the Inspector needs to advocate that responsibility is in fact necessary: 'Public men have responsibilities as well as privileges'. Similarly, Mrs Birling is hugely resistant to changing her views: 'I've done nothing wrong'. Accordingly the Inspector is harshest with her – 'I think you did something terribly wrong' – thus advocating the importance of collective responsibility in a direct and firm way.***

This shows a critical awareness of how Priestley uses his characters to make a moral/political point (A01).* However this also shows a critical response to the significance of the language with the carefully chosen quotes and the brief discussion of the significance of the language ** (AO2). It also impresses with the fluency and coherence of the writing, using discourse markers (Another way..) to signal the flow of ideas from one to the other.

> *In contrast, the younger characters readily accept their guilt, thus portraying Priestley's optimistic hope for the future. The younger generation are presented as having the capacity to build a less*

selfish society and to learn to take responsibility. Sheila, for example, readily admits her guilt: 'It's was my own fault' and accordingly the Inspector does not pass harsh moral judgement on her.

The Inspector's clearest advocation of the need for responsibility comes in Act III with his parting speech, in which he speaks of all people being 'intertwined with our lives'. He effectively uses powerful, biblical language in an effort to threaten the characters into changing: 'They will be taught it in fire and blood and anguish'. *This tone successfully persuades the audience of the need of collectivism: with the benefit of hindsight, we recognise that the Inspector is speaking prophetically about the Second World War.** Thus we realise that we could take destiny in our hands and change things   if we adopt unselfish attitudes, thus ensuring that there is not another repeat of the war.

This reveals a good grasp of the effects of the language Priestley uses here (AO2)*. However, more impressive in many ways is the complex grasp of context, acknowledging the chronological difference between the setting of the play and its reception by an audience, indicated by 'with the benefit of hindsight' (AO4). **

These ideas are clearly present at the end of the play, when some of the characters, having found out that 'that man wasn't a police inspector' and that nobody had died, assume that they can go on living as before. Gerald's revelation here was a test of what the characters had learnt, and indeed, Birling is seen to have not changed: 'The whole thing's different now'. Throughout the play, Birling has kept to his principle that 'a man has to look after *himself and his own,' illustrating his selfishness and heartlessness. Similarly Mrs Birling seems more upset by the Inspector's tone of voice than anything she learnt that evening: 'so rude – and assertive'*. At the very end, however, these characters are taught their lesson, as the Inspector prophesied, when they receive a telephone call to say that 'a Police Inspector is on his way here to ask some questions', As this is a direct repeat of the events which occurred earlier in the play, Priestley is clearly arguing that there is no escape from the responsibility of our own actions.*

This is a lovely point revealing a sensitivity to the significance of the language Mrs Birling uses (AO2).

Priestley alludes to this idea throughout the play, both by voicing his own conscience through the words of the Inspector and through the play's events as a reflection of society and the two world wars. By clearly portraying the attitudes of the elder characters as being selfish and heartless, Priestley also encourages us to adopt the attitudes of the younger ones, thus similarly advocating directly to the audience the need of collectivism.

<u>Comments</u>

- ✓ **BAND 6** - This essay achieved full marks in the English Literature GCSE.

- ✓ Fluent and well-focused style answering the question clearly. Discourse markers represent cohesion and the grammar and spelling is accurate.

✓ A critical awareness of the significance of language is displayed.

✓ Apposite quotes are used throughout the essay revealing a wide-ranging knowledge of all facets of the play.

✓ A secure knowledge of the historical context is linked directly and with imagination to the text and task.

▸ **Essay 6 explores the importance of Jack in 'Lord of the Flies'**

In 'Lord of the Flies', a group of school boys is isolated on a remote desert island. WIlliam Golding wrote the novel in 1954, having been appalled by the holocaust and the bloodshed of World War II. He now thought that evil came from inside man, normally <u>suppressed by our conscience**</u>, but he felt that as the rules of society were lost in the war, evil was released to devastating effect. <u>Thus</u>**, he explores this in 'Lord of the Flies', as the boys soon forget the rules of society and degenerate into savage and primitive men. <u>Jack is a main character in the novel and he is most important because</u> *he causes the split into two groups, and he is the <u>main atavist</u>**.

This starts with a very strong grasp of the effects of context on the text (AO4) but keeps the style succinct and clearly focusses on the question asked, at the end of the paragraph*. The style is mature and uses critical vocabulary accurately and with insight **(AO1).

Firstly,** Jack is the main fighter for power, he brings the anger and competition between himself and Ralph because he wants

*power. As he meets him he says, 'I should be chief'. He says this
with 'simple arrogance', which shows how *desperate he is to be
chief. We are also told, 'the obvious leader was Jack'; therefore**
he creates conflict when Ralph is chosen instead. The reader is
shown his despair for power as he 'clutches the conch to himself',
where the verb conveys his desperation*. By the end Jack has
become 'the chief in truth'. The importance of Jack's lust for
power is that it separates him and shows his discontentment and
thus** acceleration into degeneration.*

This develops its explanation of the significance of the language used by
the author exemplified in the highlighted phrases (AO2)*. It also uses a
succinct and well-focused style to show cohesion form one paragraph/
idea to the next **, clearly signposted by the use of connectives (such as
"therefore") .

*Secondly, and in contrast Ralph is the democratic leader on the
island. Therefore if Jack had not been there, then the outcome
would have been very different. But, as Jack was there, he played
the par tof a dictator, like Hitler, separating the island into two
groups,preying on the weak. Jack has 'red hair beneath the black
cap' and he wears a 'black coat'. These two colours, red and
black, symbolise power and evil.* As a dictator he opposes
Ralph's views and thus causes discontentment among the boys.
He challenges Ralph, saying, 'we'll have rules, lots of rule. Then,
when anyone breaks them - '. This illustrates *his dictatorness
and creates tension. Later in the novelRoger says, 'he's a proper
chief' because he is beating up WIlfred. Hence Jack represents
tyranny*, which contrasts with Ralph's democratic ideals. This
conflict leads to savagery.*

*This candidate reveals sophisticated awareness of the effects of the author's choice of imagery and its symbolism. (AO2) *. All points are backed up with wide ranging and apposite quotes from throughout the novel revealing an excellent grasp of the main themes (AO1).*

Moreover, Jack seems to the human form of evil, the human face of the devil. He persuades the 'littluns' to believe in fear, not to forget it as Simon tries to say. He does this so that he can run a tribe of boys who will fight fear - if there was no fear then the boys wouldn't need the tribe. Therefore, he exploits the situation to fit with his regime, like Hitler. Also, he is represented as a companion of the beast. Golding writes, 'and the ape chattered into his air'. This is like the beast since it is referred to as an 'ape-like creature'. So, Jack is important because he exaggerates fear and the beast in order to rule a tribe, which he desperately wants. Without Jack, the boys could have forgotten about fear and maybe stayed closer to society.*

Furthermore, Golding wanted to write a novel in which he could express his attitudes to humans degenerating to a primitive state**. Thus he uses Jack to illustrate the process. A choir leader and public schoolboy, in the beginning he is boxed in by the rules of society. So he failed to kill the first time because of 'the enormity of the knife descending and cutting into living fresh...' However*, he does kill and after reverts to savagery. He paints a mask onto his face under which he could hide from the 'shame and self-consciousness' which he had been experiencing. He's important, therefore, as he is the first character to degenerate and*

Golding can easily** use him to show the easy slip into savagery.

A secure style is clearly structured through the use of discourse markers and connectives*(AO1). This answer shows a very astute understanding of the ways the author has constructed his text to make a certain psychological point and the style puts the focus on the craft of the author ** (AO2).

In addition to degeneration, Jack is also responsible for the separation of the boys on the island. He is the first to disagree with Ralph and the only one to discredit the rules: 'B******s to the rules'. Crucially it is also Jack who changes the chant from 'kill the pig' to 'kill the BEAST'. This is to insert fear into the boys' minds and make them easy to control.

Jack is therefore a very important character in the novel. He is the cause of fear, savagery and the separation of the boys into tribes. Most importantly he leads their degeneration. Without him Ralph would have remained a democratic leader and thus the boys would have stayed with clear rules of society. In Freudian terms Jack allows the 'Id' to be exposed and thus allows the animal primitive ways to triumph of the 'ego' of reason. Finally, Merridew means 'Lord of the Mace' andGolding allows him to live up to his name.

Comments

✓ This is a very strong, top Band 6.

✓ Highly sophisticated understanding of the ways the author has crafted the text for effect.

✓ An excellent grasp not only of the historical context of the text , but also of the ways this applies to and influences the text.

✓ Well-structured style uses discourse markers confidently and the expression reveals highly developed critical skills.

✓ The whole text is covered in the time showing a detailed knowledge of the text and managing to make critical points in some depth.

▸ **Essay 7 focuses on 'triviality' in 'The Importance of Being Earnest'**

'The Importance of Being Earnest' is essentially a comedy of manners, where Wilde ridicules the Victorian society which surrounds him. Wilde's voice shines clearly through the text of the play and through characters such as Algernon. As a person Wilde believed in the importance of aestheticism. This love of beauty and decadence can be seen in the satirical and ironic lines that hold a revealing mirror to the audience, who valued strength of character and prized ' the moral duty'. Thus, Wilde's trivial play is actually rather a play revealing the triviality of the 'serious issues'.

The characters in Wilde's play all have an element of ridicule. Perhaps one of the most important characters to show this is Jack Worthing. As discovered in the play, Jack's alter-ego is a fictitious man named Earnest Worthing. In the play there is a quest to acquire the title or name of Earnest. It is a quest for the name, but not the actual, real, moral attribute of earnestness.

For example, as Gwendolen states "my ideal has always to been to love someone of the name Earnest". It is said that the name inspires 'absolute confidence'. However, in this situation Wilde reveals a truth that one should not judge based upon a name. Earnest Worthing does not exist and Jack's adoption of the name is purely so he can visit London and escape his moral duties. A further aspect of the name to note is the superficial nature of the surname "Worthing". While the sound of the name is similar to the adjective 'worthy', on deeper examination it can be seen to not bear the weight of that characteristic. Worthing is a seaside resort in Sussex. Such a place alludes to a place of leisure, where moral conduct is lowered. Thus, in this way, Wilde gives names to his characters that prove not to match with their personalities. Therefore, he is suggesting that Victorian society is obsessed with acquiring titles and labels or certain virtues like earnestness, yet the titles are superficial and it turns out that the characteristics are not possessed.

In terms of language, Wilde cleverly inverts well known phrases, subverting their conventional meanings. On the surface they appear paradoxical, but on further examination one finds that this ironic technique reveals certain truths about the state of Victorian society. For example, Algernon states "Divorces are made in heaven". This statement can be seen to be rather blasphemous as it is disregarding the loving intentions of God and the purpose of unity. However, it reflects the state of England in the late 19th century. The country was struggling for identity and to remain a shining icon to the World. However, as seen from the line said by Algernon, Society was in confusion and even something that is *opposed by the Church has become something that is permitted by God.*

This can be further emphasised by the literary context of the day. The novel 'Doctor Jekyll and Mr Hyde' displays the split in personality and the degeneration of the human mind. In 'The Importance of Being Earnest' Wilde conveys this split through the act of 'bunburying'. The principal characters lead secret or double lives, where they can escape from the moral strictness of public behaviour. Even their public behaviour can be a mask of manners, hiding their true feelings. While the Victorian era had a calm, earnest superficial exterior, Wilde reveals that there was a corrupt interior.

Finally, Wilde touches upon the idea of the 'new woman'. Strong characters such as Gewndolen try to break free from their controlling mothers. A further example is the reference to Lady Harbury who instead of turning white with grief over the death of her husband has turned 'quite gold'. This alludes to the oppression of women during this time. On the other hand, Wilde makes characters such as Lady Bracknell unsympathetic.

Overall, Wilde is creating an iconic portrayal of society which, when held up to the audience, appears to be a trivial likeness. But in the shadows of the language, lurk the dangers and the actual state of society.

✓ This is a fluent, sophisticated essay, demonstrating a very good understanding of literary and socio-historical contexts and of the play.

✓ The candidate develops a number of convincing points, moving freely over the text to support their ideas.

✓ Though a little limited, the analysis of language is astute. Band 6, low A*.

▸ **Essay 8 focuses on love and marriage in 'Pride and Prejudice'**

From the opening sentence of "Pride and Prejudice", the central theme of marriage is introduced. For many modern readers, this is naturally as a result of love; however the presence of love is not always a requisite in the novel's marriages and is important in determining the characters' lives and happiness.

Clearly, the character of Charlotte Lucas is "not romantic" and so believes one can be happy without love and respect for one's partner:

"Happiness in marriage is entirely a matter of choice."

On Lizzie's visit to Hunsford Parsonage, she observes that Charlotte attempts to make the best of her situation, without necessarily possessing any love and respect for her "rather insensible" husband.

Furthermore, Jane Austen also suggests that "love" is a feeling which cannot be based purely on superficial looks - this is proven by the marriage of Mr and Mrs Bennet:

"Her father, captivated by youth and beauty....had married a woman whose weak understanding and illiberal mind had very early put an end to all real affection..."

Without the presence of anything more substantial than "affection" based on "youth and beauty", the Bennets' marriage is a weak one; Mr Bennet's need to retire to his library for solitude and peace proves that, without love, he cannot really be content with his situation.

Perhaps, then, Jane Austen's view on the importance of love is expressed via her centre of consciousness and fellow ironist, the heroine Lizzie:

"I love him. I do, I do..."

In order to constitute the happy union of Lizzie and Darcy, love and understanding is required – as Jane comments, "do anything but marry without affection". In stark contrast to the marriages of Mr and Mrs Bennet and Lydia and Wickham, it is clear that Lizzie and Darcy do go on to be happy.

However, through the elongated and, for the reader, frustrating courtship of Elizabeth and Darcy, it is clear that their love for one another is a result of mutual respect and understanding. As Mr Bennet comments:

"Lizzie, I know you could not be happy without esteem for your partner."

Unlike the superficial understanding Lydia and Wickham (and most probably Mr and Mrs Bennet) have for one another after a marriage based on lust and appearance, the road to Elizabeth and Darcy's marriage is like the road to Pemberley House described by Austen as "long and winding". They have both had the opportunity to find out whether they do really respect the other, and so disprove Charlotte Lucas' theory that "happiness in marriage is entirely a matter of choice". In this way, Austen seems to indicate that love is important for a happy marriage, and the reader is led to question whether this is why she turned down the economically convenient proposal of a wealthy businessman, who it is clear she had no love for.

However, it is not true to say that love is the only factor contributing to the success and happiness of Austen's characters, or that love is based solely on mutual respect and understanding. When questioned by Jane about when she first fell in love with Darcy, Lizzie replies:

"I believe I must date it from my first seeing his beautiful grounds at Pemberley."

Although it is clear that Lizzie, along with Mr Bennet and the narrator, is one of the novel's ironists, the reader cannot help but detect a hint of truth in her words – perhaps, it is possible for love to be based on material possessions rather than character to a degree. However, the successful marriage of Lizzie and Darcy (and that of Jane and Mr Bingley to an extent) does prove the need for "love" in order to constitute happiness, however it may have been formed.

In conclusion, in a novel in which the characters experience greatly varying degrees of happiness, Jane Austen makes it clear that love is an important factor in determining the strength of affection for one's partner. Love, in the view of Lizzie and the narrator, is also very important in determining the happiness of a marriage – many of "Pride and Prejudice"'s least successful marriages are formed from lust, superficial first appearances or for economical stability. Most importantly perhaps, it is clear that love comes only as a result of mutual respect and time to find out about one's partner – in this way, Lizzie and Darcy provide the novel's perfect example of a loving couple.

<u>Comments</u>

✓ Band 6.

✓ Grade- Solid A*.

✓ This has a strong grasp of the complexities of both text and task(AO1).

✓ The approach to the question is focussed throughout and reveals a mature awareness of the multifarious ways in which this question can be approached (AO1).

✓ The candidate reveals their understanding of the author's craft in a few strong examples, and apposite quotes are used to back up points(AO2). The depth of knowledge of the novel is strong as shown by this focussed quotation throughout.

✓ The style is clear and has some flair at points.

Now it's your turn to be the examiner. What grade would you give this? See if you can use the **AOs** to explain your reasons.

▸ **'Bonus' Essay, on 'An Inspector Calls**

"An Inspector Calls" was written by J. B. Priestley at a time of social and political upheaval – first shown in 1946, it came straight after World War 11, a catalyst for change, and the election of a Labour Government.

For this reason, Priestley's play is almost Brechtian style – he uses stereotypical characters such as Mr Birling to represent the shortcomings of a capitalist, uncaring attitude. From Mr Birling's involvement in the life of Eva Smith, it is clear that he believes his workers to be "cheap labour", almost unworthy of classification as people with feelings:

"It's my duty to keep labour costs down...so I refused."

Mr Birling is one of a sector of Upper-Middle Class society who had elevated their position by means of business and trade. In this way, his derogatory attitude is a result of his own desire to maintain and strengthen his social standing and for this reason his treatment of Eva Smith is, to a more modern audience, unfair and repulsive.

Mrs Birling, in many ways, extends further on such a view of the lower classes. Coming from landed gentry, her attitudes to Eva Birling are snobbish and derogatory:

"She was claiming elaborate fine feelings and scruples that were simply absurd in a girl in her position."

In this way, Mrs Birling stereotypically represents a whole sector of society even more extreme in their attitude than Mr Birling - believing herself to be by far the social superior of the working classes (represented by Eva Smith), Mrs Birling believes Eva to have almost a sub human status.

Clearly, through creating the grotesques of Mr and Mrs Birling as a mockery for the audience, it is obvious that Priestly disagrees with such attitudes to social status. His views are far more socialist and caring, and for this reason he needs to create characters capable of proving his own views to be correct.

In the play, this role is fulfilled by the Inspector – through his omniscience, calmness and authority, the Inspector is able to prove the faults of the Birlings' Edwardian, capitalist attitudes and express Priestley's own far more socialist perspective:

"We don't live alone. We are members of one body. We are responsible for each other."

In the Inspector, Priestly creates a character whose omniscience and omnipotency draw the audience along to his perspective – in this way, the Inspector creates a battle between socialism and the

Birlings' capitalism in which Priestley's own socialist view is naturally the victor.

Through the younger Birling generation, Priestley gives a glimmer of hope for the audience. Unlike their parents and Gerald Croft, Eric and particularly Sheila seem capable of changing their view, as Sheila is able to condemn her parents' uncaring attitude:

"You began to learn something. And now you've stopped. You're ready to go on in the same old way."

The fact the younger generations are capable of change is significant – through Sheila and Eric, Priestley symbolises the changing attitude of a post-war audience who should, and have to some degree, learnt from the "fire and blood and anguish". At the time, Priestley was one of many authors who attempted to capture a public change of opinion and changing attitudes to social status which were in sharp contrast to the fixed, Edwardian Capitalist views of the Birling family.

Furthermore, cyclic nature of the play is part if its didactic nature – Priestley aims to teach the audience the faults of the Birlings' attitude. At the beginning of the play, the Inspector calls after a girl dies at the infirmary – at the end of the play, Mr Birling receives a phone call to say "A girl has just died….a police inspector is on his way". Through this, Priestley expresses his belief that history will just carry on repeating itself unless society can learn from the mistakes of its attitude to social status – and, for those who refuse to change (such as the Birlings), they will continue to make mistakes and cause harm such as the death of

Eva Smith.

In conclusion, it is clear that Priestley expresses the more socialist views prevalent in a society whose attitude to social status were changing. Through Eva Smith's painful and unnecessary death (in which the whole Birling family are involved), Priestley proves the faults of the Edwardian, Capitalist attitudes of the time the play was set (1912). However, through his own mouthpiece (the Inspector) and the younger generation who are capable of change, Priestley conveys the changing social attitudes of the post WW11 society to which the play was performed. The play indicates that if only everybody could be converted to Priestley's view, there would be no more unnecessary deaths such as that of Eva Smith.

Ten Top Tips on writing a great GCSE Literature Essay

1. Know throughly the assessment objectives and how they are weighted on specific essays.

2. Examine the two aspects of all texts; what they are about and how they are written.

3. Break the texts down into further key aspects; language, sound effects, emotional tone, structure and so forth. Consider how these contribute to the exploration of the text's themes.

4. Brainstorm, plan and sequence your points.

5. Set out a clear introduction and your line of argument. Start with one of your strongest points.

6. Make sure you answer the question set by advancing about 5 or 6 points. Start each paragraph with a point.

7. Use PEA (POINT-EXAMPLE-ANALYSIS) to develop and prove these. Make sure you use at least one quotation per paragraph and that you analyse the language in all your quotes.

8. Write in an academic formal style using the correct technical vocabulary. Unless you're expressing the impact of the poem on you, avoid using the first person (I think, I feel); use instead the depersonalised voice. Make sure that if you are writing about a play that you show you know it is not a novel. The quickest way to do this is by writing about how the audience might respond.

9. Leave time to check your essay before you hand it in

10. Try to enjoy writing your essay and to make it interesting for the reader. If you're bored by what you're writing and the way that you're expressing yourself, it's likely that your reader will be bored too. A lively engaging style will carry you a long way.

CONCLUSION

If you've read this far and managed all the exercises you will have greatly enhanced your understanding of what it takes to gain A*.

Remember, writing English Literature essays at any level, GCSE, A level, Degree or Post graduate, isn't about repeating what other people have told you, or what you've read in a revision guide, or following a rigid writing frame. Of course you should inform yourself about what other people think as that will help you to test and refine your own ideas. As we've shown, you also have to understand the assessment criteria: the rules of the game.

Fundamentally your essays should be your own, expressing your own ideas, in your own voice, in your own unique way. Different people will read poems in different ways. The examiner wants to know what you think. Before you write your next Literature essay, take a deep breath, embrace the freedom and try to express yourself as clearly, persuasively and interestingly as you can.

At the start of this book we used a sporting analogy.

We see you now going out onto the games field, dressed in all the right kit. You've practised all the key skills so that you're adept at all of them. You completely understand all the rules of the game. You feel confident, but not cocky, because you know precisely what you're doing. You have every chance, because of the thoroughness of your preparation, of playing the best game of your life.

And, when the match is finally over, unsurprisingly, your performance on the field has indeed been truly outstanding.

Edexcel, AQA and Cambridge IGCSE mark schemes

(WJEC's can be found on the board's website.)

Instead of repeating a summary, for the following examples from Edexcel and Cambridge IGCSE mark schemes we have highlighted the most significant words and added a sentence at the end to clarify.

EDEXCEL CONTROLLED ASSESSMENT MARKING CRITERIA

As with AQA Edexcel's marking criteria for controlled assessment stretches from Band 1 to 5. The bands only roughly approximate to grades.

Band 3

- **SOUND** explanation of how the writer uses language, structure and form to create effect

- **SOME CLEAR UNDERSTANDING** of how language, structure and form contribute to presentation of ideas, themes or settings

- The selection of examples is appropriate; shows **SOME SUPPORT OF THE POINTS** being made

- Sound comparisons and links

- **SOME CLEAR** evaluation of the different ways of expressing meaning and achieving effects

(In other words at around a C level, though there is clear understanding of texts essays are not very developed or detailed.)

Band 4

- Specific and **DETAILED EXPLANATION** of how the writer uses language, structure and form to create effect

- **DEVELOPED UNDERSTANDING** of how language, structure and form contribute to presentation of ideas, themes or settings

- The selection of examples is detailed, appropriate and supports the points being made

- Specific and detailed comparisons and links

- **DEVELOPED EVALUATION** of the different ways of expressing meaning and achieving effects

- **COMMUNICATES IDEAS EFFECTIVELY** using correct terminology and organises material clearly. Spelling, punctuation and grammar will be mostly accurate

So moving up the grade ladder from a C to a B is achieved by writing in more detail about themes and techniques. For a B grade you also have to explain how writers use language to achieve effects.

Band 5

- **DISCRIMINATING** comparisons and links showing **INSIGHT**

- **PERCEPTIVE EVALUATION** of the different ways of expressing meaning and achieving effects

- The selection of examples is **DISCRIMINATING;** fully supports the points being made

- Communicates ideas effectively using appropriate terminology and organises material **COHERENTLY**

- Spelling, punctuation and grammar will be accurate throughout

- **DISCRIMINATING EXPLANATION** of how the writer uses language, structure and form to create effect

- **PERCEPTIVE UNDERSTANDING** of how language, structure and form contribute to presentation of ideas, themes or settings

For AQA and most other boards band 5 is the top band, and band 1 is the lowest. For some reason the Cambridge IGCSE uses 1 to equal the top band and 7 to indicate the lowest band. Again we have highlighted the crucial phrases.

AQA - CONTROLLED ASSESSMENT CRITERIA

Band 3

'CLEAR, CONSISTENT': Responses in Band 3 will be expected to show clear and consistent engagement with a range of ideas and techniques.

Candidates demonstrate:

- Clear understanding of writers' ideas and use relevant and appropriate supporting textual detail

- Clear understanding of features of language and structure supported by relevant and appropriate quotation

- Clear and balanced understanding of links/points of comparison between texts

- A clear grasp of the significance of some aspects of the contexts.

Band 4

'CONFIDENT, ASSURED': Responses in Band 4 will be expected to show assured engagement with a broad range of ideas and techniques.

Candidates demonstrate:

- Sustained and developed appreciation of writers' ideas and attitudes and provide convincing interpretations using precisely selected supporting textual detail

- Analysis of aspects of language and structure in convincing detail

- Thoughtful and balanced consideration of links/points of comparison between the texts

- Thoughtful consideration of the significance of the contexts

Band 5

'SOPHISTICATED, IMPRESSIVE': Responses in Band 5 will be expected to show sophisticated engagement with a broad range of ideas and techniques.

Candidates demonstrate:

- Sophisticated engagement with writers' ideas and attitudes.

- Sophisticated interpretations of texts using imaginatively selected supporting textual detail

- Sophisticated analysis of aspects of language and structure

- Perceptive, imaginative and balanced exploration of points of linkage/comparison

- Perceptive and imaginative comment on the significance of the contexts

The most important information is summarised in the following way:

- **GRADE C** - Demonstrates a clear, competent understanding of the themes and techniques of the texts studied

- **GRADE B** - Demonstrates a developed appreciation of the themes and techniques of the texts studied

- **GRADES A/A*** - Demonstrates a sophisticated analysis of the themes and techniques of the texts studied

CAMBRIDGE IGCSE COURSEWORK MARKING CRITERIA

Band 7

- Some evidence of simple personal response

- Makes a few straightforward comments

- Shows a few signs of understanding the surface meaning of the text

- Makes a little reference to the text

Band 6

- Attempts to communicate a basic personal response

- Makes some relevant comments

- Shows a basic understanding of surface meaning of the text

- Makes a little supporting reference to the text

Band 5

- Begins to develop a personal response

- Shows some understanding of meaning

- Makes a little reference to the language of the text (beginning to assume a voice in an empathic task)

- Uses some supporting textual detail

Band 4

- Makes a reasonably developed personal response

- Shows understanding of the text and some of its deeper implications

- Makes some response to the way the writer uses language (using suitable features of expression in an empathic task)

- Shows some thoroughness in the use of supporting evidence from the text

Band 3

- Makes a well-developed and detailed personal response

- Shows a clear understanding of the text and some of its deeper implications

- Makes a developed response to the way the writer achieves her/his effects (sustaining an appropriate voice in an empathic task)

- Supports with careful and relevant reference to the text

Band 2

- Sustains a perceptive and convincing personal response

- Shows a clear critical understanding of the text

- Responds sensitively and in detail to the way the writer achieves her/his effects (sustaining a convincing voice in an empathic task)

- Integrates much well-selected reference to the text

Band 1

- Answers in this band have all the qualities of Band 2 work, with further insight, sensitivity, individuality and flair. They show complete and sustained engagement with both text and task.

Postscript & Acknowledgements

Neil Bowen has been teaching English for about 15 years, working in both the state and independent sectors. Currently he is Head of English at Wells Cathedral School in sunny Somerset. He has written many articles on English Literature and a number of popular teaching resources for 'A' level. Recently he has started a Masters Degree in Literature and Teaching at Cambridge University.

Neil created and runs the literature website, peripeteia.web.com.

I would like to say a big 'thank you' to my colleague, Harriet Brown, who read drafts of this book, made helpful suggestions for its improvement and also provided some of the excellent examiners' commentaries. And, of course, a big 'thanks' too to my students, whose (mostly excellent) work I have quoted extensively in this book.

Printed by BoD™in Norderstedt, Germany